ITALIAN STREET FOOD

ITALIAN STREET FOOD

{ RECIPES FROM ITALY'S BARS
AND HIDDEN LANEWAYS }

PAOLA BACCHIA

Smith
Street
Books

CONTENT

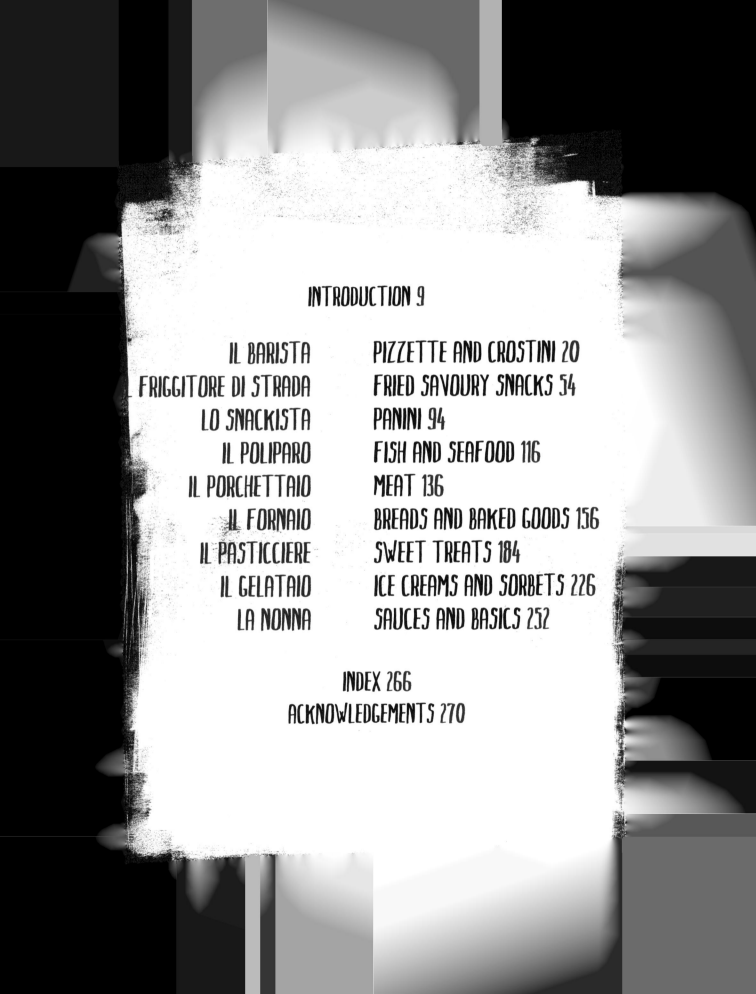

INTRODUCTION 9

IL BARISTA	PIZZETTE AND CROSTINI 20
IL FRIGGITORE DI STRADA	FRIED SAVOURY SNACKS 54
LO SNACKISTA	PANINI 94
IL POLIPARO	FISH AND SEAFOOD 116
IL PORCHETTAIO	MEAT 136
IL FORNAIO	BREADS AND BAKED GOODS 156
IL PASTICCIERE	SWEET TREATS 184
IL GELATAIO	ICE CREAMS AND SORBETS 226
LA NONNA	SAUCES AND BASICS 252

INDEX 266

ACKNOWLEDGEMENTS 270

INTRODUCTION

As a child, I cannot remember a weekend when mamma's meat sugo was not bubbling on the stovetop – garlic, pork, beef and tomato all melding into the most amazing rich meaty scent that wafted through the fly-wire door and onto the street. The neighbours would find a reason to drop by to see my mother, Livia, in her kitchen and maybe get a chance to taste what she was cooking. When papa was not at work, he was in his garage, concocting wine or grappa, or in the garden growing fruit and vegetables that our neighbours had never heard of, such as radicchio, which mamma would then turn into a simple savoury masterpiece and place on the dinner table each night. Papa always admonished us to 'know where your food comes from' and that 'no one cooks as well as your mother does'. And we just listened to his mantra, nodding while we ate. But he was right, the wise man that he was. We knew that the food we ate came from his garden, picked a couple of hours earlier, or from the Italian butchers and grocers who he knew by name. It also came from the heart, specifically mamma's Veneta heart – all that maternal love was poured into caring for her family through good quality, seasonal, regional Italian food.

Food is central to the Italian way of life – I have never met an Italian who did not mention food in almost every conversation, describing what their last meal or *spuntino* (snack) was or what their next one will be, invariably with a strong opinion on the dish. And just like my father had repeated to me, for the average Italian, their mamma is the best cook, maybe only surpassed by *nonna* (grandmother) before she hands on the baton (or wooden spoon) to the next generation. Region, provenance and seasonality always matters to them, so it stands to reason that street food in Italy combines all of these elements; if it didn't, Italians probably wouldn't eat it.

{ FAST FOOD VS. STREET FOOD }

What is Italian street food? Let me tell you what it is not: fast food. It is tasty, often cheap, but has a story and a tradition. A popular street food sold from vans in Florence, *panino con lampredotto*, is a sandwich filled with cow innards, specifically the stomach, which is cooked at length until tender in a broth with various vegetables and herbs. Florentines adore these panini, which are soaked briefly in the cooking broth, then filled with thinly sliced meat and sometimes topped with a herb-based salsa verde. They stand around the vans at lunchtime, sipping small glasses of Tuscan red wine, tucking into their delicious panini, before heading off to continue their work day. To me, this doesn't fit with what we might call fast food in English, which has connotations of added sugars, fats, mass production and 'sameness', where customers are happily assured of the same-tasting product no matter where in the world it is bought.

Authentic Italian street food puts you in touch with the local people who make it, their land, their traditions, their ancestors and even their mothers. It is as much about geography as it is about tradition; what grows locally and is plentiful is more likely to be a key part of a particular dish. A traditional *porchetta* (roast pork) roll made by an artisan *porchettaio* (porchetta-maker) in Abruzzo will probably taste different from a porchetta roll eaten in Umbria. It might be made with different herbs (wild fennel in Umbria and rosemary in Abruzzo), the pig will have been raised on different land with different feed, and there will be some secret ingredient or cooking method handed down from mamma (or another family member equally qualified in the kitchen) that makes their porchetta better than everyone else's.

Don't get me wrong – you can also find mass-produced fast food on the streets of Italy, in particular in larger towns and cities, where the busy tourist trade far outstrips local artisanal production. However, if you follow a local along the street and down a narrow laneway, even in those large towns, you will find the artisan food producer, inspired by what they learned in their home kitchen, cooking authentic traditional and regional food to be eaten on the streets, in the laneways or in the bars using the traditions handed down from his or her ancestors.

The eating of street food follows the rhythms of the day. Mornings begin with a pastry and coffee eaten standing up or with elbows on the counter of the bar. The next stop might be a mid-morning visit to the fornaio for a slice of focaccia, and later for those who are unable to get back home for the traditional long leisurely lunch, a lunchtime panino with a small glass of wine, taken standing up outside the paninoteca or next to a food van. Mid afternoon might find you walking the streets in search of an ice-cream cart and later on, in time for the apertivo hour, you might select a plate of crostini in a bar or one of the many types of vegetarian or meat polpettine. In the evening, hungry young night-clubbers search for kiosks selling skewers of arrosticini or bombette, or cones of fried fish.

It is these recipes that you will find in this book; recipes which tell a story and stem from traditions, adapted for home cooking and using ingredients that are readily available. Making food at home is one of my greatest joys and to make traditional foods that take me back to the streets of Italy is the next best thing to being there.

{ ITALIAN STREET FOOD: A BRIEF HISTORY }

Food has been made, purchased and eaten on the streets of Italy for a very long time. Thanks to the eruption of Mount Vesuvius in 79 AD, we can trace street food in Italy back to the days of Pompeii. We know that the thermopolium sold wine and hot food stored in terracotta pots, waiting for customers to arrive. This ancient version of a take-away was for those who did not have kitchens in their own homes or those who perhaps enjoyed heading out for a convivial meal and a wine while catching up with friends. Food would be eaten standing up, while walking along one of the Roman streets or in the little dining rooms that were sometimes found at the back of the thermopolium.

In the late 1800s, as recounted by Italian food writer, Carlo Valli, the Italian piazza was not only the place to meet and exchange news, it was the cultural and trade centre of the town, where money was exchanged for goods and food. Street sellers were at its heart and street food was what fed the community. Valli describes street food vendors that specialised in one thing, and so had specific skills and corresponding titles. Some titles that are no longer in use include *il ranaiolo*, who caught frogs and prepared and sold them in bunches; *il lumacaio*, who caught and sold both live and cooked snails dressed with parsley, garlic and oil; and *il brustolinaio*, who prepared and sold roasted salted pepitas (pumpkin seeds), a kind of precursor to popcorn. You can still find a number of street food vendors with the same traditional names, selling their food on Italian streets: *il caldarrostaio*, who sells *caldarroste* (roasted chestnuts); *il trippaio*, who sells cooked tripe piled into bread rolls on the streets of Florence; and *il meusaro*, who prepares and sells cooked *milza* (spleen) on the streets of Palermo. As the language and roles have transformed over time, new roles have developed based on a globalised view of food and the words that describe it, such as *lo snackista*, who prepares snacks – mainly small sandwiches – in bars.

Photographs taken in the late 1800s on the streets of Naples provide evidence of a bustling street food culture. This was a time when the city was densely populated, housing was at bursting point, many homes did not have kitchens and through necessity, people lived a large part of their lives on the street. The photos depict black and white scenes of *zeppole* being fried in large vats of oil, *taralli* being sold on trestle tables in markets and plates of spaghetti being prepared, dried out, cooked and then eaten on the streets by hordes of hungry Neapolitans. This was a time of great

poverty and when pizza, with a simple topping of tomatoes, garlic, pepper and oregano prepared by the *pizzaiuolo* (pizza maker), was breakfast and lunch for a large part of the population.

Now of course, nearly all houses have kitchens where food is prepared by mamma, but life is still lived outdoors in many cities and towns, especially in the less industrialised south of Italy including Naples. If you walk along the narrow streets you will see washing hanging on lines strung between rows of tall apartment houses; women talking to each other from windows on opposite sides of the laneway; groups of men standing or sitting on makeshift seats made of crates on the street playing Italian cards. Food still plays a central role and

there continues to be a thriving street food scene, not only to feed tourists, but to satisfy hungry locals, who for the necessities and pace of modern-day life, cook less at home and eat out more. In the historic Ballaro market in Palermo, you can buy panelle or arancini for just over €1, cooked for you on the spot in a huge vat of bubbling spitting oil; their fragrance wafting through the market stalls. The *friggitore da strada* (street fryer) scoops them out with a long-handled slotted spoon and hands them to you in a paper napkin, and you eat them standing up or walking through the streets of this vibrant and intriguing market.

In the town of Bari Vecchia (the walled old city), older women sit just inside their homes with the door open, so passers-by can peer in and see them deftly rolling orecchiette from a semolina-based pasta dough. The orecchiette are left out to dry under a thin mesh curtain on makeshift trestle tables in the street and later sold to locals as well as tourists, who want to enjoy handmade and hand-rolled traditional pasta.

{ ITALIAN STREET FOOD: FOOD VANS, FAIRS AND BARS }

Italian street food delivered from vans and mobile kiosks has enjoyed a resurgence in recent years. The economic crisis of 2008 resulted in the closure of many shops and restaurants, with a concurrent slow but steady increase in the number of mobile food vendors. The mobility, flexibility and lower running costs of vans means that street food costs are kept low, making it a great way to eat out but not spend a fortune. As a result, street food sold from small vans (often the 3-wheeled *Ape* – pronounced 'ah-peh', meaning 'bee' – made by the manufacturer Piaggio) or larger outfitted trucks have become increasingly popular for younger people, who enjoy the social aspect of the experience as much as the food.

The popularity of street food is linked to the worldwide phenomenon that started in the USA. In Italy, rather than it being called *cibo da strada* (which translates to 'food of the street'), the English term 'street food' is often used (or even the phonetic spelling of *strit fud*) with several websites dedicated to sharing news and events, and connecting Italians who are interested in street food. There are many annual street food festivals around Italy – in the first half of 2016, there were over 25 festivals scattered around the peninsula alone. Although some sell American-style foods such as *hamburger di pollo* (chicken burger) or *panini con pulled pork* (pulled pork roll), the majority have a focus on regional and traditional food. The long history of street food vendors in Italy bears testament to the fact that rather than being the adoption of an overseas trend, it is very much an adaptation of an Italian tradition.

Sagre (fairs) are traditional festivals with a religious origin that are a celebration of the land and what it produces, held in the streets, the *piazze* (town squares) and in parks. They are traditional to the place where they are held, often with a long-standing history, and celebrate a particular ingredient or product. Examples include *sagra del pesce* (fish fair); *sagra degli asparagi* (asparagus fair); and *sagra del fungo porcino* (porcini mushroom fair). Food is a highlight of *sagre* which often stretch over a number of days. Meals are sold from vans and stalls which highlight the ingredient that is at the centre of the feast.

Bars in Italy are nothing like their Australian or British counterparts. The Italian bar is more like a café serving small bites of sweet and savoury food, coffee and wine, and is a meeting place for locals, as an extension of the traditional *piazza* (town square). If you have been to Italy and get the sense that there is a bar on every corner, well there almost is.

In 2012 there were over 172,000 bars in Italy. This huge number means that a large proportion of smaller snacks, including breakfast *brioche* (pastries), late-morning *pizzette* (mini pizze) or aperitif-time *crostini* (bread-based mini snacks with toppings), are consumed in a bar, while standing or sitting on stools or at tables outside. The bar is not a place to linger – a quick coffee, drink, a snack and a chat with friends, and you are on your way.

{ ITALIAN STREET FOOD: THE RECIPES }

Last year, I went on a whirlwind tour up and down the length of Italy to hunt down the tastiest and most authentic street foods. Three weeks of eating, talking to vendors and making notes led me to the definition of street food that I have used in this book. It can be mostly eaten without cutlery (although you might use a skewer or toothpick) and can be eaten on the run but also sitting in or standing at a bar. It is food that might be cooked on the spot or transported to the place where you are eating it, from a *pasticceria* (pastry shop) or *forno* (bakery). It might be purchased from a kiosk, van, or from a small bar or a shop, usually outwards facing, with an opening onto the street or close to it, in a town, or at a fair. It might be typical of a time of the year, or associated with a religious festival, or particular to a town or region. It is generally not more than a few mouthfuls and is often eaten *in fretta* (in a hurry).

Not all of the street food that I found can be replicated at home. On the way to the Archaeological Museum in Naples last year, I came across a cart selling *pizza a portafloglio*, which literally means 'note-carrying' or 'wallet' pizza because of how it is folded over, so that the topping doesn't fall out. The crust was thick and chewy, the centre thin and covered with sweet tomatoes and a sprinkling of oregano – it was masterfully simple and perfect. This perfection is almost impossible to obtain at home because most of us do not have the wood-fire oven required to recreate it. Thus, although I have included *pizzette* (which are tiny snack-sized pizze you might eat in an Italian bar) in the barista section of this book, I have not included pizza itself.

The ingredients used in *Italian Street Food* are few and recipes focus on the more traditional cooking methods such as frying and baking. There are many breads and other smaller bites that make ideal appetisers, party finger foods and go well with a glass of Prosecco or a beer. I have given myself a bit of creative freedom in the gelato chapter, as any good *gelataio* (ice-cream maker) would do, and have experimented with new flavour combinations or tried to recreate flavours I tasted during my Italian travels.

NOTES ON INGREDIENTS

{WHEAT FLOURS}

Wheat flour is classified by its protein (or gluten) content or by how finely the flour has been milled. What you plan to use the flour for will guide which one you should select.

PROTEIN CONTENT

This is important because it dictates how much water the flour absorbs, how much it stretches and therefore what it can be used for. In general, the higher the protein content, the longer the proving time and the more the dough will stretch. Occasionally, you may find a packet of flour that has a W followed by a number. This describes the exact amount of protein present in the flour – W360 is a high protein content flour, whereas W120 is a low protein content flour. Most flour, however, is simply labelled with a description rather than a precise protein content.

Much of flour that you buy in the shops is made from the grains *Triticum aestivum* or *Triticum durum*. Flour packaging will generally state whether the flour is 'strong' and 'hard' or 'soft' and 'weak'. Strong flour indicates that it has a high protein content and is generally suitable for breads and pizze. Italian flour labelled 'Manitoba' is a strong flour. For more delicate cakes and pastries, 'soft' or 'weak' flour is generally used. This flour has a lower gluten content.

All-purpose plain flour is just that, a good all-rounder with a medium protein content. It is suitable for most recipes except for where it specifically asks for flour that is 'strong' or 'weak'.

FLOUR MILLING

Many Italian recipes call for 00 flour. This describes how finely the flour is milled. 00 flour is very fine and very white.

If the label does not describe the 00 flour as being 'strong' or 'weak', you can assume it is an all-purpose finely milled flour. However, Italian flour brands often specify whether the 00 flour is suitable for cakes (i.e. weak) or for breads and pizze (i.e. strong).

Type 0 flour tends to be darker in colour as it is less finely milled. You can usually substitute plain (all-purpose) flour; however, if it is prefaced by the word *duro* (hard), then use strong flour.

Semolina is the yellow coarsely ground endosperm of *Triticum durum* and is therefore also made from wheat. *Semola* looks like polenta and is often used to make pasta. *Semola rimacinata* has been re-ground and looks very much like regular flour. It is sometimes labelled 'semolina flour' or 'fine' semolina. It is used to make certain types of pasta and pizza, often in combination with finer flours.

{YEAST}

Many of the recipes in this book are bread-based and use yeast. At home, I often use fresh yeast, however, I know that it is not always convenient to have this in the fridge and it loses its ability to rise after a few weeks (despite what the use-by label might say). That said, it can be frozen with satisfactory results. A good alternative to fresh yeast is instant dried yeast. This type of yeast has a fine granule and can be mixed directly into the flour. It comes in a container that should be sealed and kept in the fridge. Always check the use-by date as it loses its rising ability over time. Do not confuse instant dried yeast with active dried yeast. The latter has a coarser granule and therefore must be dissolved in water first, meaning that if you use it you may have to alter the methodology of your recipe.

In converting a recipe from fresh yeast to instant dried yeast, I use the general rule of multiplying the amount of fresh yeast by 0.4. For example, 20 g (¾ oz) of fresh yeast equals 5 g (¼ oz) of instant dried yeast. When using dried yeast, it makes a difference if you use a few grams more or less. Recipes may not work as intended if you do not use the precise amount. So, using a teaspoon to measure dried yeast can be problematic. One metric teaspoon of dried yeast weighs just over 3 g (⅛ oz). So, if a recipe calls for 5 g (¼ oz) of dried yeast, it is a bit tricky to convert this accurately to a teaspoon. I always weigh all my dry ingredients and having a precise digital scale is essential when using dried yeast. It might take a few more minutes but when baking breads or cakes, you cannot afford imprecision.

{ CHEESES }

Cheese is one of the staples of Italian cooking. Think of how many recipes use mozzarella, ricotta, parmesan – Italian food just wouldn't be the same without it. Many of the recipes in this book contain cheese and those that are used in Italian cooking can be a bit different from the ones you might find on your local delicatessen or supermarket shelf. They might have the same name but they can differ to what you would find on the shelf in Italy.

RICOTTA

Ricotta (literally meaning 're-cooked') is made from milk whey (traditionally sheep's milk) and is a by-product of making other cheeses. It is white, fluffy, slightly sweet and very versatile. You can make it at home by heating very fresh milk and adding a bit of vinegar until the milk curdles. Much of the ricotta you buy in Australia is made from cow's milk rather than sheep's milk. Commercially, rather than being a by-product of cheese-making, most ricotta is made from whole milk with an added acid.

I am lucky enough to have a local cheese producer where they make fresh cow's milk ricotta daily. As an alternative, I buy the ricotta that comes in its own draining basket from a supermarket or by weight from a delicatessen. It has a delicate taste and is quite firm. And it is creamy not grainy. It can be easily whipped to make it smooth and spreadable. Some packaged ricotta has gums and stabilisers added, making it easy to spread, however this alters its structure, generally making it grainy and chalky. This type of packaged ricotta is not suitable for cooking, as it tends to turn into a wet mess. All of the recipes in this book that call for ricotta are made using fresh cow's whole milk ricotta, bought from the supermarket in its own draining basket.

MOZZARELLA

Mozzarella is made by the *pasta filata* (stretched curd) method traditionally with *latte di bufala* (buffalo milk). *Fior di latte* (literally meaning 'flower of milk') is made by a similar stretched curd method and is sometimes used interchangeably with mozzarella, but differs in that it is made with cow's milk. As cow's milk has a lower fat and protein content compared to buffalo milk, its properties are quite different, with buffalo mozzarella being wetter and a bit slower to melt.

Mozzarella can be purchased fresh or aged. In cooking, mozzarella is ideal for dishes that require melted cheese with a mild taste. When Italians refer to mozzarella, they generally mean the fresh buffalo mozzarella, which has a milky colour and is soft, wet and stored in brine. To confuse matters further, fresh mozzarella can also be made with cow's milk but at least in Italy, you will know what it is made from, as it will be clearly labelled. In terms of shape, fresh mozzarella is typically ball-shaped with one flat side.

Mozzarella that you find on the supermarket shelf that comes in a vacuum-sealed pack without brine (and is what a lot of people think of as mozzarella) has been aged with much of the moisture removed. It is generally made with cow's milk, has a rubbery texture and excellent melting properties. It is fine to use on pizza or Pizzette (page 24) or if making lasagna or Panzerotti (page 79); however, I wouldn't recommend eating it on its own with bread, as it is rather bland and the texture is somewhat unpleasant. As an alternative to what I refer to as aged/regular mozzarella, you can use scamorza, another stretched curd cheese made with cow's milk. Scamorza is an aged fior di latte and if produced by an artisan, is far superior to supermarket-bought regular mozzarella. Scamorza can be white (*scamorza bianca*) or smoked (*scamorza affumicata*) and its delicate flavour and firm (but not rubbery) texture make it suitable for eating on its own with bread.

The recipes in this book use fresh mozzarella (buffalo mozzarella, fior di latte or bocconcini) or aged mozzarella (scamorza or regular mozzarella). Choose whichever is easiest to find, noting that fresh mozzarella is always wetter than aged mozzarella.

IL BARIST

{ PIZZETTE AND CROSTINI }

PIZZETTE

Pizzette con pomodoro e mozzarella
Tomato and mozzarella pizzette

Pizzette con patate e cipolle
Potato and onion pizzette

Pizzette con pomodoro e acciughe
Tomato and anchovy pizzette

Pizzette con Gorgonzola e funghi
Gorgonzola and mushroom pizzette

Pizzette con salsicce, zucchine e mozzarella
Sausage, zucchini and mozzarella pizzette

CROSTINI

Crostini con uova sode e acciughe
Crostini with egg and anchovy

Crostini con Gorgonzola, pera e balsamico
Crostini with Gorgonzola, pear and balsamic

Crostini con ricotta mantecata, acciughe e frutti del cappero
Crostini with whipped ricotta, anchovy and caperberries

Crostini con radicchio sottaceto e bresaola
Crostini with pickled radicchio and bresaola

Crostini con crema di sgombro e capperi
Crostini with mackerel pâté and capers

Crostini con burro, acciughe e mozzarella
Crostini with butter, anchovies and fresh mozzarella

My *zio* (uncle) Mario has been a regular at Bar alla Posta for about 30 years. It's where he goes to get his morning coffee and pastry, play a quick game of *Briscola* (a popular Italian card game) with friends at the tables on the sidewalk, a late afternoon *spuntino* (snack) and an aperitif, and where he returns on the rare occasions he decides to have a nightcap. Prior to that, Mario and his friends went to Bar al Commercio, which is three doors along and closer to the piazza, but they made the move when the barista left il Commercio to start working at la Posta. That kind of loyalty is rare, but a clear demonstration of the strong relationship between the barista and his patrons.

Many Italians, particularly those who are retired, spend a lot of time at their local bar. It is a familiar second home, complete with other regulars and the barista, who become members of an extended family. They proffer opinions on the weather, the comings and goings of the neighbourhood and of course, food. Visits to a bar might be a few times a day, but they are seldom long: a quick coffee or drink, a small snack, a quick chat to the barista and the other customers, and you are on your way.

In Italy, the role of the barista is a bit different from baristas elsewhere in the Western world (which is often limited to coffee-making). The classic Italian barista works behind the bar, making coffee, but also takes on the role of barman, serving alcoholic and soft drinks and preparing and/or serving snacks from pastries to *pizzette* (mini pizze). The food served at these Italian bars is often regional – you are unlikely to find tiny open bread sandwiches (*crostini*) in a bar in Sicily for example, but they are sold widely in bars in Florence and Venice.

Venice deserves a special mention because, in addition to regular Italian-style bars, there are also a large number of *bacari*, which are more akin to wine bars. Bacari specialise in wine and accompanying bite-sized savoury snacks called *cichetti*, and are often set up as small hole-in-the-wall establishments. Given that Venice is on a lagoon, many cichetti are seafood-based, such as *sarde in saor* (sardines in a sweet–sour sauce), and are often served on rounds of crostini. They can also include bite-sized *polpette* (meatballs) made with seafood, meat or eggplant.

On my last visit to Venice, I found a tiny bacaro (called a *bacareto*) off the beaten track in Campo dei Tolentini. It opened at 8 am and served small glasses of wine from jugs labelled nero and bianco and tiny panini called *topolini* (little mice) with either prosciutto, salame or cheese. At 10 am when I walked past, there were at least a dozen people standing outside, with drinks of wine perched on old wine barrels, eating their topolini. I fought my way into the narrow bar and ordered exactly what the others were having from the barista, who was juggling jugs of wine and food as well as collecting money. A couple of men were out the back, assembling more food. On a misty and cold day in Venice, it seemed just about perfect.

PIZZETTE

{ BASIC PIZZETTE DOUGH }

BASIC DOUGH

500 G (1 LB 2 OZ) PLAIN (ALL-PURPOSE) FLOUR

10 G (⅓ OZ) INSTANT DRIED YEAST

1 TEASPOON OLIVE OIL

250 ML (8½ FL OZ/1 CUP) TEPID WATER

1½ TEASPOONS SALT

40 G BUTTER, AT ROOM TEMPERATURE, CUT INTO SMALL CUBES

Walk into a bar on an afternoon in Italy, and you will nearly always see pizzette piled high in the display window. Usually topped with tomato and mozzarella cheese, these bite-sized mini pizze make a great accompaniment to a late afternoon or early evening glass of wine. They are also simple to make at home, and are a huge hit with the kids. I bake them on a pizza stone, which I keep in the oven while it is heating. It is the next best thing to having your own wood-fired oven and they are readily available from most good kitchenware stores.

You can vary the toppings on your pizzette and serve them as an antipasto at dinner parties. There are five varieties in this chapter, but please experiment with your favourite pizza ingredients. Just remember the rule of keeping it simple and seasonal – and no more than three toppings on a single pizzetta. There are no quantities for the ingredients – it depends entirely on how many pizzette you are making. When I make the full quantity of dough, I make three or four types of pizzette in a production line.

Combine the flour and yeast in a large bowl, then tip onto a clean work surface. Make a well in the centre and gradually add the olive oil and water. Work the flour into the liquid using a fork, starting from the centre and moving outwards, until you have a rough dough.

Add the salt and a few cubes of butter and work them into the dough by kneading. Keep adding cubes of butter until it is all incorporated and the dough is smooth. Place in a large bowl, cover with plastic wrap and place in a draught-free spot for at least 1 hour or until doubled in size.

Choose from the recipes on the following pages to cook the pizzette.

MAKES 30 x 8 CM (3¼ IN) PIZZETTE

PIZZETTE con POMODORO e MOZZARELLA

{ TOMATO AND MOZZARELLA PIZZETTE }

PLAIN (ALL-PURPOSE) FLOUR, FOR DUSTING
BASIC PIZZETTE DOUGH (PAGE 24)
EXTRA-VIRGIN OLIVE OIL
400 G (14 OZ) TINNED CHOPPED TOMATOES
DRIED OREGANO
AGED OR REGULAR MOZZARELLA OR SCAMORZA
(SEE PAGES 18–19), CUT INTO SMALL CUBES
SEA SALT FLAKES

Preheat the oven to 220°C (430°F) and place a pizza stone on a high shelf.

On a lightly floured work surface, roll out the dough, flipping it around and over every now and then until you get a roundish shape. Using an 8 cm (3¼ in) cookie cutter, cut out circles of dough. Using your finger, rub each circle with a little olive oil.

Make a shallow and broad well in the centre of each circle. Place a heaped teaspoon of chopped tomatoes in the well and top with a pinch of oregano.

Carefully transfer the pizzette to the pizza stone and bake for 6 minutes. Remove the stone from the oven and place on a heatproof surface. Scatter the cubed mozzarella on the pizzette, then slide the stone back into the oven and bake for a further 6 minutes or until the dough is golden and the cheese is melted.

Drizzle a little extra-virgin olive oil on each pizzetta, sprinkle over some sea salt flakes, to taste, and serve warm.

PIZZETTE con PATATE e CIPOLLE

{ POTATO AND ONION PIZZETTE }

PLAIN (ALL-PURPOSE) FLOUR, FOR DUSTING

1 MEDIUM-SIZED POTATO (PONTIAC OR DESIREE)

BASIC PIZZETTE DOUGH (PAGE 24)

EXTRA-VIRGIN OLIVE OIL

¼ SMALL RED ONION, THINLY SLICED

A FEW ROSEMARY SPRIGS, LEAVES PICKED

SEA SALT FLAKES

Preheat the oven to 220°C (430°F) and place a pizza stone on a high shelf.

Place the potato in a small saucepan of salted water over medium heat and boil until tender. Drain, peel and thinly slice.

On a lightly floured work surface, roll out the dough, flipping it around and over every now and then until you get a roundish shape. Using an 8 cm (3¼ in) cookie cutter, cut out circles of dough. Using your finger, rub each circle with a little olive oil.

Place 1–2 slices of potato on each pizzetta, then top with a few onion slices and a couple of rosemary leaves.

Carefully transfer the pizzette to the pizza stone and bake for 12 minutes or until golden.

Drizzle a little extra-virgin olive oil on each pizzetta, sprinkle over some sea salt flakes, to taste, and serve warm.

PIZZETTE con POMODORO e ACCIUGHE

{ TOMATO AND ANCHOVY PIZZETTE }

PLAIN (ALL-PURPOSE) FLOUR, FOR DUSTING

BASIC PIZZETTE DOUGH (PAGE 24)

EXTRA-VIRGIN OLIVE OIL

400 G (14 OZ) TINNED CHOPPED TOMATOES

ANCHOVIES IN OLIVE OIL, DRAINED AND THINLY SLICED

CAPERBERRIES, DRAINED

Preheat the oven to 220°C (430°F) and place a pizza stone on a high shelf.

On a lightly floured work surface, roll out the dough, flipping it around and over every now and then until you get a roundish shape. Using an 8 cm (3¼ in) cookie cutter, cut out circles of dough. Using your finger, rub each circle with a little olive oil.

Make a shallow and broad well in the centre of each circle. Place a heaped teaspoon of chopped tomatoes in the well and top with a few slices of anchovy.

Carefully transfer the pizzette to the pizza stone and bake for 6 minutes. Remove the stone from the oven and place on a heatproof surface. Place a caperberry on top of each pizzetta, then slide the stone back into the oven and bake for a further 6 minutes or until the dough is golden.

Drizzle a little extra-virgin olive oil on each pizzetta and serve warm.

PIZZETTE con GORGONZOLA e FUNGHI

{ GORGONZOLA AND MUSHROOM PIZZETTE }

SPLASH OF OLIVE OIL

1 GARLIC CLOVE, PEELED AND BRUISED

SWISS BROWN BUTTON MUSHROOMS, WIPED CLEAN AND THINLY SLICED

A FEW THYME SPRIGS, LEAVES PICKED, PLUS EXTRA, TO SERVE

PLAIN (ALL-PURPOSE) FLOUR, FOR DUSTING

BASIC PIZZETTE DOUGH (PAGE 24)

EXTRA-VIRGIN OLIVE OIL

GORGONZOLA OR OTHER CREAMY BLUE CHEESE, SLICED

SEA SALT FLAKES

Heat the olive oil and garlic in a small frying pan over medium heat. When the garlic becomes fragrant, add the mushrooms and cook, stirring, for a few minutes, then reduce the heat and add a few thyme leaves. Simmer until the mushrooms have softened, adding a splash of water if they become too dry. Add salt and pepper, to taste, and set aside.

Preheat the oven to 220°C (430°F) and place a pizza stone on a high shelf.

On a lightly floured work surface, roll out the dough, flipping it around and over every now and then until you get a roundish shape. Using an 8 cm (3¼ in) cookie cutter, cut out circles of dough. Using your finger, rub each circle with a little olive oil.

Place a slice of Gorgonzola on each pizzetta followed by a small pile of cooked mushrooms.

Carefully transfer the pizzette to the pizza stone and bake for 12 minutes or until golden.

Drizzle a little extra-virgin olive oil on each pizzetta, sprinkle over some sea salt flakes, to taste, and garnish with a sprig of thyme. Serve warm.

PIZZETTE con SALSICCE, ZUCCHINE e MOZZARELLA

{ SAUSAGE, ZUCCHINI AND MOZZARELLA PIZZETTE }

PORK AND FENNEL SAUSAGES (1 SAUSAGE WILL BE ENOUGH FOR ABOUT 10 PIZZETTE)

PLAIN (ALL-PURPOSE) FLOUR, FOR DUSTING

BASIC PIZZETTE DOUGH (PAGE 24)

EXTRA-VIRGIN OLIVE OIL

THINLY SLICED ZUCCHINI (COURGETTE)

AGED OR REGULAR MOZZARELLA OR SCAMORZA (SEE PAGES 18–19), CUT INTO SMALL CUBES

Remove the skins from the sausages and transfer the meat to a small bowl. Mash with the back of a fork until you have a crumb-like consistency. Transfer to a small non-stick frying pan, and cook over medium heat for about 5 minutes, until cooked through. Set aside.

Preheat the oven to 220°C (430°F) and place a pizza stone on a high shelf.

On a lightly floured work surface, roll out the dough, flipping it around and over every now and then until you get a roundish shape. Using an 8 cm (3¼ in) cookie cutter, cut out circles of dough. Using your finger, rub each circle with a little olive oil.

Place 2–3 slices of zucchini on each pizzetta, then top with a teaspoon of the cooked sausage meat.

Carefully transfer the pizzette to the pizza stone and bake for 6 minutes. Remove the stone from the oven and place on a heatproof surface. Scatter the cubed cheese over each pizzetta, then slide the stone back into the oven and bake for a further 6 minutes, or until the dough is golden and the cheese is melted.

Drizzle a little extra-virgin olive oil on each pizzetta and serve warm.

CROSTINI

Crostini are little rounds of toasted day-old bread, usually cooked on a grill and topped with all manner of delicious things. They are typically eaten in the late afternoon, often with a glass of wine, standing up at a bar or perched on a barstool. They are typical of Tuscany and Umbria as well as Venice, where they are one of the many cichetti (snacks) you can find at bacari or osterie.

When I make crostini at home, I brush the bread lightly with olive oil and then grill on a chargrill pan until charred lines appear. You should be guided by what you like best – fresh bread, day-old bread or grilled bread – the topping is what I believe matters the most. I tend to use a sourdough breadstick, as the size is just about right for crostini. You can also serve the bread just grilled and warm, or at room temperature – it is up to you. I like to grill the bread about 10 minutes before serving.

Here are six of my favourite crostini toppings. They make a lovely appetiser for when guests drop by. Most of the toppings can be prepared well in advance, so all you have to do is assemble them (or have one of your guests help you, while you both have a glass of wine).

CROSTINI con UOVA SODE e ACCIUGHE

{ CROSTINI WITH EGG AND ANCHOVY }

1 SMALL BREADSTICK OR BAGUETTE, CUT INTO 1 CM (½ IN) THICK SLICES

OLIVE OIL, FOR BRUSHING

2 HARD-BOILED EGGS, PEELED

24 GOOD-QUALITY ANCHOVIES

CHILLI FLAKES

GOOD-QUALITY EXTRA-VIRGIN OLIVE OIL

This may sound very simple, but the combination of hard-boiled eggs and anchovies is divine. Make sure you use the best anchovies you can find (Spanish anchovies have a very good reputation and generally speaking, the more expensive, the better) as well as a good-quality olive oil for drizzling on the crostini. The quality of these key ingredients really makes a difference.

Brush the slices of bread with a little olive oil and place on a chargrill pan. Cook over a high heat until chargrill lines appear, then turn over and cook the other side, ensuring that the bread doesn't burn. This can be done several hours in advance or just before serving if you would like the crostini to be slightly warm.

Slice the hard-boiled egg into 2–3 mm (⅛ in) rounds. Top each crostino with 1–2 egg slices (depending on the size of your bread), 2 anchovies, a sprinkling of chilli flakes and a drizzle of extra-virgin olive oil.

Place a toothpick through the centre of each crostino (optional) and serve.

MAKES 12

CROSTINI con GORGONZOLA, PERA e BALSAMICO

{ CROSTINI WITH GORGONZOLA, PEAR AND BALSAMIC }

1 SMALL BREADSTICK OR BAGUETTE, CUT INTO
1 CM (½ IN) THICK SLICES

OLIVE OIL, FOR BRUSHING

60 ML (2 FL OZ/¼ CUP) BALSAMIC VINEGAR

120 G (4½ OZ) GORGONZOLA OR SIMILAR
CREAMY BLUE CHEESE

1–2 RIPE PEARS, PEELED, CORED AND SLICED

The combination of creamy piquant blue cheese, sweet pears and sweet but sour balsamic vinegar is heavenly. Make sure the pears are ripe but firm – beurre bosc work very well. You can substitute a ready-made balsamic glaze if you do not want to make your own balsamic reduction.

Brush the slices of bread with a little olive oil and place on a chargrill pan. Cook over a high heat until chargrill lines appear, then turn over and cook the other side, ensuring that the bread doesn't burn. This can be done several hours in advance or just before serving, if you would like the crostini to be slightly warm.

To make a balsamic reduction, pour the balsamic vinegar into a small saucepan over medium heat. When it starts to simmer, reduce the heat to low and cook for 8–10 minutes, until the vinegar has reduced to a thick syrup. Remove from the heat and set aside to cool.

Crumble a little blue cheese on each crostino, top with a few slices of pear and drizzle over some of the balsamic reduction.

Place a toothpick through the centre of each crostino (optional) and serve.

MAKES 12

CROSTINI con RICOTTA MANTECATA, ACCIUGHE e FRUTTI DEL CAPPERO

{ CROSTINI WITH WHIPPED RICOTTA, ANCHOVY AND CAPERBERRIES }

1 SMALL BREADSTICK OR BAGUETTE. CUT INTO 1 CM (½ IN) THICK SLICES

OLIVE OIL. FOR BRUSHING

180 G (6½ OZ) RICOTTA (SEE PAGE 18)

12 GOOD-QUALITY ANCHOVIES

12 CAPERBERRIES (OR 36 SALTED CAPERS, RINSED)

Ricotta is amazingly versatile. By whipping it in a food processor you can make a creamy crostino topping in next to no time. I like to put it in a piping bag (you can make your own by using a small zip lock bag and snipping off one of the corners). You can substitute rinsed salted capers for the caperberries, but I like the long stem that looks a little bit like a tail.

Brush the slices of bread with a little olive oil and place on a chargrill pan. Cook over a high heat until chargrill lines appear, then turn over and cook the other side, ensuring that the bread doesn't burn. This can be done several hours in advance or just before serving, if you would like the crostini to be slightly warm.

Place the ricotta in a mini food processor and process for about 15 seconds until it turns into a thick cream. (This can be done ahead of time and set aside in the fridge until you are ready to assemble the crostini.) Transfer the ricotta cream to a piping bag, and pipe a small mound onto each slice of grilled bread. Wrap an anchovy around the ricotta, top with a caperberry (or 3 capers) and serve immediately.

MAKES 12

CROSTINI con RADICCHIO SOTTACETO e BRESAOLA

{ CROSTINI WITH PICKLED RADICCHIO AND BRESAOLA }

5 RED RADICCHIO LEAVES

60 ML (2 FL OZ/¼ CUP) PROSECCO OR DRY WHITE WINE

60 ML (2 FL OZ/¼ CUP) WHITE WINE VINEGAR

2 JUNIPER BERRIES

2 PEPPERCORNS

½ TEASPOON SUGAR

EXTRA-VIRGIN OLIVE OIL

1 SMALL BREADSTICK OR BAGUETTE, CUT INTO 1 CM (½ IN) THICK SLICES

OLIVE OIL, FOR BRUSHING

12 SLICES BRESAOLA

My local delicatessen stocks wagyu bresaola, which is a cut above regular air-dried beef. It is also quite a bit more expensive, but infinitely superior in quality – it is heavily marbled and melts in your mouth. It makes a great contrast to the slightly bitter pickled red radicchio. If you cannot find bresaola, a thinly sliced good-quality salame makes a perfectly good substitute. You will have more pickled radicchio than you need (it will make enough for about 24 crostini). Store it in the fridge for a few days, well covered in olive oil, in a sealed container.

To make the pickled radicchio, wash and dry the radicchio leaves. Cut into thin strips, and remove the toughest part of the white stem. Place the Prosecco or dry white wine, vinegar, juniper berries, peppercorns and sugar in a small saucepan and bring to the boil. Remove from the heat and drop in the radicchio leaves, submerging them as much as possible. Set aside to soak in the liquid for 5 minutes, then drain and transfer to a small bowl and cover with extra-virgin olive oil.

Brush the slices of bread with a little olive oil and place on a chargrill pan. Cook over a high heat until chargrill lines appear, then turn over and cook the other side, ensuring that the bread doesn't burn. This can be done several hours in advance or just before serving, if you would like the crostini to be slightly warm.

Place a slice of bresaola on each crostino and top with a few strips of pickled radicchio.

Place a toothpick through the centre of each crostino (optional) and serve.

MAKES 12

CROSTINI con CREMA DI SGOMBRO e CAPPERI

{ CROSTINI WITH MACKEREL PÂTÉ AND CAPERS }

1 SMALL BREADSTICK OR BAGUETTE, CUT INTO 1 CM (½ IN) THICK SLICES

OLIVE OIL, FOR BRUSHING

120 G (4½ OZ) TINNED GOOD-QUALITY MACKEREL, DRAINED

½ TABLESPOON EXTRA-VIRGIN OLIVE OIL

1 EGG YOLK

½ TEASPOON WHITE WINE VINEGAR

125 ML (4 FL OZ/½ CUP) VEGETABLE OIL

SEA SALT FLAKES

A FEW CORAL OR BUTTER LETTUCE LEAVES, FINELY CHOPPED

SALTED CAPERS, WELL RINSED

The mackerel 'crema' in this recipe is essentially a mackerel mayonnaise. Make sure you use good-quality tinned mackerel in olive oil, preferably from Italy or Spain. Look for salted capers rather than those in brine, which can have a vinegary taste. Remember to rinse them well or they will be excessively salty. I usually soak them for about 5 minutes in a small bowl of water to remove the excess salt.

Brush the slices of bread with a little olive oil and place on a chargrill pan. Cook over a high heat until chargrill lines appear, then turn over and cook the other side, ensuring that the bread doesn't burn. This can be done several hours in advance or just before serving, if you would like the crostini to be slightly warm.

Pop the drained mackerel into a mini food processor. With the motor running, drizzle in the extra-virgin olive oil (or used the drained olive oil from the can) and process until the mackerel is spreadable, thick and homogenous. Set aside.

Place the egg yolk and vinegar in a medium-sized bowl. Using an electric whisk or hand-held beaters, whisk briefly to break the egg yolk. Continue to whisk vigorously and slowly drizzle in the vegetable oil in a steady stream – this should take about 1 minute. The mixture will thicken and turn into mayonnaise. Add sea salt flakes, to taste.

In a separate bowl, combine equal quantities of mayonnaise and mackerel paste (you will have some mayonnaise left over).

Place a small pile of lettuce on each crostino, then add 1 teaspoon of mackerel pâté and a few capers. Season with freshly ground black pepper, to taste, and serve.

MAKES 12

CROSTINI con BURRO, ACCIUGHE e MOZZARELLA

{ CROSTINI WITH BUTTER, ANCHOVIES AND FRESH MOZZARELLA }

1 SMALL BREADSTICK OR BAGUETTE, CUT INTO 1 CM (½ IN) THICK SLICES

OLIVE OIL, FOR BRUSHING

GOOD-QUALITY UNSALTED ITALIAN OR FRENCH BUTTER

FRESH BUFFALO MOZZARELLA OR FIOR DI LATTE (SEE PAGE 18), SLICED

12 GOOD-QUALITY ANCHOVIES

To achieve a truly authentic taste, it is important to use the best-quality ingredients you can find for these crostini. Spanish anchovies are generally of excellent quality and I always use Italian butter, which is very pale and creamy. French butter or local cultured butter is a good substitute.

Brush the slices of bread with a little olive oil and place on a chargrill pan. Cook over a high heat until chargrill lines appear, then turn over and cook the other side, ensuring that the bread doesn't burn. This can be done several hours in advance or just before serving; however, the crostini should be served at room temperature, so that the butter doesn't melt.

To assemble the crostini, spread a thick layer of butter on each crostino, top with a slice of fresh mozzarella and an anchovy, then serve immediately.

MAKES 12

iL FRiGGiTO
Di STRAD

{ FRIED SAVOURY SNACKS }

Polpettine di melanzane
Eggplant polpettine

Supplì al telefono con ragù
Supplì with meat ragù

Arancini con pomodoro e piselli
Arancini with tomatoes and peas

Coccoli fritti
Fried bread balls

Mozzarella in carrozza
Fried mozzarella sandwich

Fiori di zucchini ripieni
Stuffed zucchini flowers in batter

Crochette di patate
Potato croquettes

Panzerotti
Fried dough pockets

Polpette di cicoria
Chicory polpette

Frico
Potato and cheese pancake

Scagliozzi
Polenta chips

Zeppole con acciughe e olive
Zeppole with anchovies and olives

Panelle
Chickpea fritters

Mozzarella fritta
Fried mozzarella balls

In Palermo there are four open-air markets that fan out from the Baroque Quattro Canti. These vibrant historic markets are loud, colourful and filled with stalls that sell the freshest fish, meat and whichever fruits and vegetables are in season. The warm climate of Sicily means that locals spend much of their time outdoors, catching up with old friends, passing the time of day, playing card games and consuming lots of local street foods such as arancini or *frittole Palermitane* (pieces of otherwise discarded veal meat and cartilage, typical of Palermo and a testament to not wasting anything). Huge vats of oil sit on stalls in the markets, bubbling away at just under boiling point, waiting for a customer to order some *panelle* (chickpea fritters). The beauty of buying panelle at the market is that they are cooked while you wait, skilfully flipped and turned in the hot oil so that they become crisp on the outside but remain soft in the middle.

The *friggitore* (fryer), or more correctly, *friggitore di strada*, is the person who fries food and sells it on the street (*strada*). Frying is one of the most popular methods of cooking outdoors, as it requires little more than a source of heat and a pot of oil (or more commonly in the past, *strutto*, which is a type of pork fat).

Everything tastes better when freshly fried and Italian street sellers have turned open-air frying into an art. Friggitori are found all over the Italian peninsula, but they were particularly common in Naples in the 1800s, and the *friggitoria* (fried food or chip shop) continues to be a permanent part of that local street food culture. The historic centre of Naples is dominated by small friggitorie with counters that face directly onto the Spaccanapoli – the street that literally splits Naples in two. Not only do they sell traditional Neapolitan fried food such as *pizza fritta* (fried pizza, where the dough circle is folded over to contain fillings and then fried) and potato croquettes but also *frittatina di pasta* (fried pasta), which is an excellent way to use up leftovers.

In the Neapolitan friggitorie you may hear the word *cuoppo*, or *cono* (cone): a receptacle for all types of fried food, traditionally made of straw. You can buy a *cono mare* (cone of the sea) or a *cono terra* (cone of the land) and eat this delicious street food as you walk around, using a bamboo skewer to retrieve the fried morsels of food from the base of the cone.

POLPETTINE di MELANZANE

{ EGGPLANT POLPETTINE }

2 MEDIUM EGGPLANTS (AUBERGINES)

1 EGG, LIGHTLY BEATEN

40 G (1½ OZ) PARMESAN CHEESE, GRATED

40 G (1½ OZ) BREADCRUMBS, PLUS EXTRA
TO CRUMB

10 MINT LEAVES, FINELY CHOPPED

PINCH OF SALT

GRAPESEED, PEANUT OR SUNFLOWER OIL,
FOR FRYING

The word 'polpetta' translates to meatball (and the diminutive polpettina is a tiny meatball). However, in Italian you can describe the word further by saying what the polpetta is made of. So, polpettine di melanzane means eggplant meatballs, which doesn't really make sense as there is no meat in them! I have eaten eggplant polpette at a **bacaro** *(bar) in Venice as well as from a street vendor in Sicily. The Sicilian version had mint leaves, which I've included here. You will need to start this recipe a day ahead.*

Preheat the oven to 180°C (350°F).

Place the eggplants on a roasting tray, prick a couple of times with a fork, then roast for about 45 minutes, until the eggplants feel tender when prodded. Set aside to cool slightly and when cool enough to handle, make a slit from the stem to the base. Scoop out the flesh and transfer to a fine-meshed sieve. Push the eggplant pulp with the back of a spoon to drain as much liquid as possible from the cooked flesh. Place the sieve over a bowl and set aside to drain overnight in the fridge.

The next day, squeeze the flesh to release any remaining liquid (you should have about 250 g/9 oz drained eggplant), then chop finely. Transfer to a large bowl and add the egg, parmesan, breadcrumbs, mint leaves and salt. Mix well with a spoon to combine.

Wet your hands and make golf ball-sized polpettine with the mixture before rolling them gently in the extra breadcrumbs. If the mixture doesn't hold together, add a few more breadcrumbs and re-roll them.

Heat enough oil for deep-frying in a small saucepan or deep-fryer to 180°C (350°F). Test the temperature of the oil by dropping in a cube of bread. If it starts to turn golden in 5 seconds, the oil is ready. Carefully place a few polpettine in the oil without overcrowding the pan and cook, turning regularly, for 4 minutes. Drain on kitchen towel and set aside while you cook the remaining polpettine. (You can also make them ahead of time and gently reheat in a microwave before serving.)

Serve warm as an appetiser. These are so moist and tasty they do not need a dipping sauce.

MAKES 14—16

SUPPLÌ al TELEFONO con RAGÙ

{ SUPPLÌ WITH MEAT RAGÙ }

110 G (4 OZ) AGED OR REGULAR MOZZARELLA OR SCAMORZA (SEE PAGES 18–19)

1 EGG (ONLY IF NECESSARY)

GRAPESEED, PEANUT OR SUNFLOWER OIL, FOR FRYING

RISOTTO

500–750 ML (17–25½ FL OZ/2–3 CUPS) BEEF STOCK (PAGE 260) OR YOUR FAVOURITE STOCK, PLUS EXTRA IF NECESSARY

2 TEASPOONS OLIVE OIL

2 TEASPOONS UNSALTED BUTTER

1 SMALL BROWN OR WHITE ONION, FINELY CHOPPED

200 G (7 OZ) CARNAROLI OR ARBORIO RICE

125 ML (4 FL OZ/½ CUP) DRY WHITE WINE

150 G (5½ OZ) LIVIA'S MEAT SUGO (PAGE 265), OR YOUR FAVOURITE PASTA SAUCE, WARMED

40 G (1½ OZ) UNSALTED BUTTER

25 G (1 OZ) GRATED PARMESAN CHEESE

CRUMB

PLAIN (ALL PURPOSE) FLOUR

2 EGGS, LIGHTLY BEATEN WITH A SPLASH OF MILK

HOMEMADE FRESH BREADCRUMBS

Supplì al telefono are Roman fried rice balls. They are oblong-shaped and generally made with leftover risotto. Supplì get their name because of the mozzarella that melts in the middle as they are cooked – the cheese forms a 'telephone line' of stretchy mozzarella as you take a bite. Although this dish is usually made with a meat ragù-based risotto, you can easily substitute your favourite vegetarian or other sauce in equal quantities and follow the same method. This recipe works best if you make the risotto the day before.

To make the risotto, bring the stock to the boil in a medium-sized saucepan.

Heat the olive oil and butter in a heavy-based saucepan over low heat. Add the onion and cook very slowly, stirring occasionally, for about 15 minutes. The onion should become translucent and soft without taking on any colour. Add the rice and increase the heat to medium–high. Toast the rice for 1–2 minutes, then add the wine. Cook, stirring, until the wine evaporates, then reduce the heat to medium and add a ladleful of stock. Continue to stir until the liquid is absorbed, then add another ladleful. Continue this process for 10 minutes.

Add the warm pasta sauce and stir well. Cook for a further 2 minutes, then season with salt, to taste. Taste the rice – it should be cooked through but still a little firm. Add a little more liquid and continue cooking, if necessary.

When you are happy with the consistency and bite of the rice, remove from the heat and stir through the butter and parmesan. Transfer to a large bowl, cover with plastic wrap and set aside in the fridge overnight.

Place the flour, egg mixture and breadcrumbs in separate shallow bowls. Cut the mozzarella into small 1 cm x 4 cm (½ in x 1½ in) batons.

With wet hands, grab a small handful of rice. Make a small well in the centre and place a baton of mozzarella in the middle. Fold the rice around it to form a smooth log shape about 4 cm x 6 cm (1½ in x 2½ in) in diameter and weighing about 55–60 g (2 oz). If the rice is not holding together, add a small egg to the rice mixture, mix well and try again.

>>

SUPPLÌ al TELEFONO con RAGÙ

Gently toss the supplì in the flour, then dip them in the egg mixture and, finally, toss in the breadcrumbs. Double-crumb by dipping in the egg and rolling in the breadcrumbs a second time. This will give the supplì a crunchy outer layer and they will be less likely to fall apart when cooking.

Heat 5 cm (2 in) of oil in a heavy-based saucepan (or use a deep-fryer) to 180°C (350°F). Test the temperature of the oil by dropping in a cube of bread. If it starts to turn golden in 5 seconds, the oil is ready. Cook the supplì in batches for 5–6 minutes, turning them regularly to ensure that they cook evenly. Drain on kitchen towel and repeat with the remaining supplì. Set aside to cool for a couple of minutes and serve warm.

MAKES 12–14

ARANCINI con POMODORO e PISELLI

{ ARANCINI WITH TOMATOES AND PEAS }

½ QUANTITY TOMATO AND PEA SALSA (PAGE 262) OR LIVIA'S MEAT SUGO (PAGE 265) FOR STUFFING

1 EGG (ONLY IF NECESSARY)

GRAPESEED, PEANUT OR SUNFLOWER OIL, FOR FRYING

RISOTTO

500–750 ML (17–25½ FL OZ/2–3 CUPS) BEEF STOCK (PAGE 265) OR YOUR FAVOURITE STOCK, PLUS EXTRA IF NECESSARY

2 TEASPOONS OLIVE OIL

2 TEASPOONS UNSALTED BUTTER

1 SMALL BROWN OR WHITE ONION, FINELY CHOPPED

200 G (7 OZ) CARNAROLI OR ARBORIO RICE

125 ML (4 FL OZ/½ CUP) DRY WHITE WINE

PINCH OF SAFFRON

40 G (1½ OZ) UNSALTED BUTTER

25 G (1 OZ) GRATED PARMESAN CHEESE

CRUMB

PLAIN (ALL-PURPOSE) FLOUR

2 EGGS, LIGHTLY BEATEN WITH A SPLASH OF MILK

HOMEMADE FRESH BREADCRUMBS

Arancini are originally from Calabria, Campania and Sicily. They are bigger than the Roman version, supplì, and are either round or cone-shaped, and often made from rice infused with saffron, which gives them their traditional yellow colour. A ragù sauce is spooned into the centre of the rice ball, rather than stirred throughout the rice (like supplì), so they need to be quite large. Traditionally, the sauce would be a meat ragù with peas, but a quicker and equally tasty way is to make a sauce with good-quality pork sausage and peas, or to make a thick pea and tomato sauce for a vegetarian version.

You will need to cook the risotto the day before making the arancini.

To make the risotto, bring the stock to the boil in a medium-sized saucepan.

Heat the olive oil and butter in a heavy-based saucepan over low heat. Add the onion and cook very slowly, stirring occasionally, for about 15 minutes. The onion should become translucent and soft without taking on any colour. Add the rice and increase the heat to medium–high. Toast the rice for 1–2 minutes, then add the wine. Cook, stirring, until the wine evaporates, then reduce the heat to medium and add a ladleful of stock and the saffron. Continue to stir until the liquid is absorbed, then add another ladleful. Continue this process for 12 minutes.

Season with salt, to taste and taste the rice – it should be cooked through but still a little firm. Add a little more liquid and continue cooking, if necessary.

When you are happy with the consistency and bite of the rice, remove from the heat and add the butter and parmesan. Transfer to a large bowl and allow to cool. Cover with plastic wrap and set aside in the fridge overnight.

Place the flour, egg mixture and breadcrumbs in separate shallow bowls.

With wet hands, grab a small handful of rice. Make a small well in the centre and place a teaspoon of your preferred sauce in the middle. Use a little more rice to cover the sauce. If the rice is not holding together, add a small egg to the rice mixture, mix well and try again. The arancini should be about 5 cm (2 in) in diameter and weigh about 55 g (2 oz). Repeat this process until all the rice has been used (you will have some leftover sauce).

»

ARANCINI con POMODORO e PISELLI

Gently toss the arancini in the flour, then dip in the egg mixture and finally toss in the breadcrumbs. Double-crumb by dipping in the egg and rolling in the breadcrumbs a second time. This will give the arancini a crunchy outer layer and they will be less likely to fall apart when cooking.

Heat 5 cm (2 in) of oil in a heavy-based saucepan (or use a deep fryer) to 180°C (350°F). Test the temperature of the oil by dropping in a cube of bread. If it starts to turn golden in 5 seconds, the oil is ready. Cook the arancini in batches for 5–6 minutes, turning them regularly to ensure that they cook evenly. Drain on kitchen towel and repeat with the remaining arancini. Set aside to cool for a couple of minutes and serve warm.

Although not traditional, you can also cook the arancini in a 200°C (400°F) oven for 25–30 minutes, turning regularly until golden.

MAKES 10

COCCOLI FRITTI

{ FRIED BREAD BALLS }

250 G (9 OZ/1²/₃ CUPS) PLAIN (ALL-PURPOSE) FLOUR, PLUS EXTRA FOR DUSTING

8 G (¹/₃ OZ) INSTANT DRIED YEAST

150 ML (5 FL OZ) TEPID WATER

½ TEASPOON SALT

GRAPESEED, PEANUT OR SUNFLOWER OIL, FOR FRYING

SEA SALT, FOR SPRINKLING

100 G (3½ OZ) FRESH STRACCHINO CHEESE (SUBSTITUTE A MILD BRIE OR OTHER SOFT CHEESE LIKE TALEGGIO, IF UNAVAILABLE), CUT INTO BITE-SIZED PIECES

16 SMALL SLICES PROSCIUTTO

Coccoli are little balls of fried bread, which I first ate in Florence at a little hole-in-the-wall shop. We ordered a small plate with a couple of vuoti (empty i.e. plain), a couple of ripieni (filled) and a couple of glasses of wine. We asked if the vuoti could be filled with a bit of stracchino *(a creamy mild fresh Italian cow's milk cheese, also known as crescenza) and then wrapped in prosciutto. This transforms the coccoli from simple to spectacular. Coccoli are best eaten warm, straight after making them, and preferably accompanied by a glass of red wine.*

Whisk the flour and yeast in a large bowl. Add the water and stir through with a wooden spoon, then add the salt. Work the dough with your hands for a few minutes until it comes together. Transfer to a lightly floured work surface and knead until smooth. Place the dough in a clean bowl, cover with plastic wrap and set aside to rest in a draught-free spot for 1 hour or until doubled in size.

Cut the dough into quarters, then divide each quarter into four and roll into little balls, covering them with a clean tea towel as you go to prevent them drying out.

Heat enough oil for deep-frying in a small saucepan or deep-fryer to 170°C (340°F). Drop a tiny piece of dough into the oil. If lots of bubbles form around the dough and it makes a sizzling sound, it's ready. Cook the coccoli in batches for 3–4 minutes, turning frequently, until light golden. Break the first one open to check that it is cooked through and adjust the temperature of the oil, if necessary. Drain on kitchen towel and sprinkle with sea salt.

Cut open the coccoli while still warm, add a little stracchino and wrap with a slice of prosciutto. Serve immediately.

MAKES ABOUT 16

MOZZARELLA in CARROZZA

{FRIED MOZZARELLA SANDWICH}

1 BALL FIOR DI LATTE (SEE PAGE 18), CUT INTO 5 MM (¼ IN) SLICES AND DRAINED FOR 10 MINUTES

8 SLICES WHITE BREAD, CRUSTS REMOVED AND HALVED INTO TRIANGLES

8 ANCHOVY FILLETS, DRAINED AND ROUGHLY CHOPPED (OPTIONAL)

PLAIN (ALL-PURPOSE) FLOUR

2 LARGE EGGS, LIGHTLY BEATEN WITH A SPLASH OF MILK

GRAPESEED, PEANUT OR SUNFLOWER OIL, FOR FRYING

SEA SALT FLAKES

Whenever I hear the term 'Mozzarella in Carrozza' I think of card games and sharing a drink with friends. It is not the type of snack you have every day, but a very popular one in the Southern Italian region of Campania. Crustless soft bread sandwiches are filled with mozzarella cheese, drenched in egg, then fried. I love adding chopped anchovies to the centre, for an extra salty taste. In Campania, fresh buffalo mozzarella is often used, but I find this too wet, so I use fior di latte, which is made from cow's milk and is therefore a bit drier.

Trim the fior di latte slices so they fit neatly on the bread triangles leaving a 5 mm (¼ in) border. Make triangle-shaped sandwiches by placing a slice of fior di latte on a slice of bread. Place an anchovy on the cheese (if using), then press another triangle of bread on top.

Place some cold water in a shallow bowl and a little flour on a plate. Dip the edges of the bread triangle briefly in the water, then dip in the flour. The flour and water will form a kind of glue to seal the edges of the triangle together. Press the edges together making sure they are well sealed. Repeat with the remaining bread, cheese and anchovies.

Divide the beaten egg between two large shallow bowls. Place the triangles in the egg, turning them over to make sure they are well coated. Leave them in the egg mixture for a couple of minutes until absorbed. Check that the edges of the sandwiches are well sealed before removing.

Heat 1 cm (½ in) oil in a large frying pan over medium heat. Add the sandwiches and shallow-fry in batches for 2 minutes or until golden on one side, then flip over and cook the other side for 2 minutes or until the cheese is melted. Drain on kitchen towel, sprinkle over a few sea salt flakes, to taste, and serve warm.

MAKES 4

FIORI di ZUCCHINI RIPIENI

{ STUFFED ZUCCHINI FLOWERS IN BATTER }

24 ZUCCHINI (COURGETTE) FLOWERS. STALKS ATTACHED

BATTER

150 G (5½ OZ/1 CUP) PLAIN (ALL-PURPOSE) FLOUR

185 ML (6 FL OZ/¾ CUP) TEPID WATER

½ TEASPOON SALT

1 EGG

GRAPESEED, PEANUT OR SUNFLOWER OIL. FOR SHALLOW-FRYING

FILLING

100 G (3½ OZ) RICOTTA (SEE PAGE 18)

1 SMALL EGG

20 G (¾ OZ) GRATED PARMESAN CHEESE

1 SCANT TABLESPOON FINELY CHOPPED MINT LEAVES

Delicate zucchini (courgette) flowers don't seem like your typical street food, however I ate them in Naples at a market where they were stuffed and freshly fried in batter, which seemed to make them remarkably robust. Finding male flowers without baby zucchini attached isn't always easy – try a farmers' market or a friendly neighbour with a big back yard who grows their own. Ricotta makes the perfect stuffing and I love combining it with fresh mint for a delicate and fresh flavour.

To make the batter, place the flour, water and salt in a large bowl and whisk until smooth. Set aside for 1 hour.

To make the filling, whisk the ricotta and egg using a fork until smooth, then fold in the parmesan and mint leaves.

Clean the flowers by gently washing them in water, then shake dry and make a cut in the side of each flower near the base. Snip off the inner stamens and place 1 teaspoon of filling (or less, depending on the size of the flower; do not over-fill) in each flower. Twist the ends and make sure the incision is well covered.

Add the egg to the batter and whisk until smooth. The batter will be quite thick and creamy.

Heat 1 cm (½ in) oil in a wide non-stick frying pan over medium–high heat.

Drop the flowers into the prepared batter, shaking lightly to remove any excess, then shallow-fry in batches, turning over after a few minutes – the flowers should be pale golden when cooked. Drain on kitchen towel and serve warm as an appetiser.

SERVES 4—6

CROCHETTE di PATATE

{ POTATO CROQUETTES }

500 G (1 LB 2 OZ) OLD FLOURY POTATOES
(DESIREE WORK WELL)

SMALL HANDFUL PARSLEY LEAVES,
FINELY CHOPPED

100 G (3½ OZ) PARMESAN CHEESE, GRATED

150 G (5½ OZ) AGED OR REGULAR MOZZARELLA
OR SCAMORZA (SEE PAGES 18–19), CUT INTO
SMALL BATONS (OPTIONAL)

2 EGGS

2 TEASPOONS MILK

GRAPESEED, PEANUT OR SUNFLOWER OIL,
FOR FRYING

CRUMB

PLAIN (ALL-PURPOSE) FLOUR

1 EGG, LIGHTLY BEATEN WITH A SPLASH
OF MILK

HOMEMADE FRESH BREADCRUMBS

Potato croquettes are typical of the friggitoria, as they are simple and inexpensive to prepare, with only one main ingredient plus a few fresh herbs. It is important to use old floury potatoes when making these at home, so that they will stick together and not fall apart during cooking. I like the combination of parmesan cheese and parsley, but mint also works well. You can also put a small baton of aged mozzarella or scamorza in the centre, which is not as traditional but I love them this way. Serve them when they are warm and I guarantee the kids (and adults) will eat them faster than you can cook them.

Place the whole unpeeled potatoes in a saucepan of cold water, cover and bring to the boil. Cook for about 30 minutes, or until tender when pierced with a fork. Drain, peel and mash or put through a potato ricer. Set aside to cool.

Place the cooled mashed potato in a large bowl with the parsley and parmesan. Season, to taste with salt and pepper and mix well with your hands.

Take a small handful of the potato mixture and shape into a log, about 5–6 cm (2–2½ in) in length. If you are using mozzarella, place a baton in the centre of the potato log and enclose with the potato. Repeat with the remaining mixture – you should get about 14 croquettes in total.

Place the flour, egg mixture and breadcrumbs in three separate shallow bowls. Roll the croquettes in the flour, dip in the egg, and then roll in the breadcrumbs, making sure the crumbs completely cover each croquette. You can repeat the layers of egg and breadcrumbs up to three times to make a thicker, crunchier crust.

Heat 4–5 cm (1½–2 in) of oil in a heavy-based saucepan (or use a deep-fryer) to 180°C (350°F). Test the temperature of the oil by dropping in a cube of bread. If it starts to turn golden in 5 seconds, the oil is ready. Cook the croquettes in batches, turning regularly, for 3–4 minutes until golden brown. Drain on kitchen paper and repeat with the remaining croquettes. Allow to rest for a couple of minutes, then serve warm for a substantial appetiser.

MAKES ABOUT 14

PANZEROTTI

{ FRIED DOUGH POCKETS }

GRAPESEED, PEANUT OR SUNFLOWER OIL, FOR FRYING

DOUGH

250 G (9 OZ/1⅔ CUPS) 00 WEAK (CAKE) FLOUR (SEE PAGE 17), PLUS EXTRA FOR DUSTING

250 G (9 OZ/2 CUPS) SEMOLINA

5 G (¼ OZ) INSTANT DRIED YEAST

250 ML (8½ FL OZ/1 CUP) TEPID WATER

3 TEASPOONS EXTRA-VIRGIN OLIVE OIL

2 TEASPOONS MILK

1 TEASPOON SALT

FILLING

800 G (1 LB 12 OZ) TINNED CHOPPED TOMATOES, WELL DRAINED

1 TEASPOON EXTRA-VIRGIN OLIVE OIL

½ TEASPOON DRIED OREGANO

350 G (12½ OZ) AGED MOZZARELLA OR SCAMORZA (SEE PAGES 18–19), DICED

Panzerotti are filled thin bread pockets typical of Puglia. They are small, deep-fried and quite addictive. One of the best places in the coastal city of Bari to buy panzerotti is il Focacciaro di Pino Ambruoso. I went there in the middle of winter and the shop was filled to bursting point with people, not only trying to get out of the cold as I had thought, but waiting for the next batch of panzerotti to be cooked. The most traditional filling is tomato and mozzarella.

To make the dough, place the flour, semolina and yeast in a large bowl and whisk briefly. Tip the mixture onto a clean work surface and make a well in the centre. Combine the water, oil and milk in a jug, then pour about half into the well. Using a fork or your fingers, start working the dry ingredients into the liquid. Slowly add the remaining liquid and continue bringing the ingredients together until it starts to form a stretchy smooth ball of dough. Sprinkle over the salt and knead the dough for a few more minutes. Transfer to a large bowl, cover with plastic wrap and set aside in a warm draught-free place for at least 1 hour or until doubled in size.

Break off 40 g (1½ oz) balls of dough and place on a floured baking tray. Cover with plastic wrap or a clean tea towel and set aside to rise for a further 30 minutes.

Meanwhile, make the filling. Place the drained chopped tomatoes, extra-virgin olive oil, dried oregano and a good pinch of salt in a bowl and give it a good stir.

On a well-floured work surface, roll out one ball of dough at a time to a 13–14 cm (5–5½ in) circle. Place 2 teaspoons of the tomato mixture in the centre and place 2 heaped teaspoons of cheese on top. Fold the dough in half to form a semi-circle, then press the edges firmly together. Pleat the edge of the dough to make a raised scalloped edge. Transfer to a lightly floured surface or some baking paper and cover with a clean tea towel. Repeat with the remaining dough and filling.

Heat 5 cm (2 in) of oil in a heavy-based saucepan (or use a deep fryer) to 180°C (350°F). Test the temperature of the oil by dropping in a cube of bread. If it starts to turn golden in 5 seconds, the oil is ready. Fry the panzerotti 1–2 at a time (depending on the size of your pan), turning once, for about 4 minutes, until golden. They will puff up quite a bit as they fry. Drain on kitchen towel and repeat with the remaining panzerotti. Serve warm.

MAKES 18–20

POLPETTE di CICORIA

{ CHICORY POLPETTE }

1 LARGE BUNCH (ABOUT 450 G/1 LB) CHICORY LEAVES

450 G (1 LB) FLOURY POTATOES, SUCH AS DESIREE

50 G (1¾ OZ) CRUSTLESS BREAD

125 ML (4 FL OZ/½ CUP) MILK

1 GARLIC CLOVE, CRUSHED

60 G (2 OZ) PARMESAN CHEESE, FINELY GRATED

HANDFUL PARSLEY LEAVES, FINELY CHOPPED

2 EGGS

½ TEASPOON SALT

½ TEASPOON FRESHLY GROUND PEPPER

PINCH OF FRESHLY GRATED NUTMEG

HOMEMADE FRESH BREADCRUMBS, FOR COATING

OLIVE OIL, FOR SHALLOW-FRYING

SIMPLE TOMATO SALSA (PAGE 261), TO SERVE

Chicory has to be one of my favorite bitter greens. The tender young leaves can be used in salads but as it gets older, the bitterness increases and it is better cooked and mixed with other ingredients. I saw these polpette in the market in Testaccio in Rome and loved the idea of turning chicory into something you can eat on the run. You could easily substitute spinach in this recipe although it won't have that characteristic bitterness.

Trim and rinse the chicory, removing any damaged leaves and cutting off the ends of the stalks. Bring a large saucepan of water to the boil and plunge the chicory in the water. Return to the boil, then immediately drain and set aside to cool. Finely chop the chicory (it will keep, covered, for several days in the fridge, if needed).

Place the whole unpeeled potatoes in a saucepan of cold water and bring to the boil. Cook for about 30 minutes or until tender when pierced with a fork. Drain, peel and mash or put through a potato ricer (you should have 350 g/12½ oz of mashed potato). Set aside to cool.

Soak the bread in the milk for a few minutes then drain and squeeze the bread. Tear into small pieces.

Place the chicory, mashed potato, bread, garlic, parmesan, parsley, eggs, salt, pepper and nutmeg in a large bowl and mix well with a wooden spoon and then with your hands if needed.

Wet your hands and roll the mixture into 30 g (1 oz) polpette. Flatten them slightly and roll in the breadcrumbs. (You can prepare the polpette up to 12 hours ahead and store, covered with plastic wrap, in the fridge).

Heat a glug of oil in a non-stick frying pan (just enough so that the surface of the pan is covered) over medium heat. Cook the polpette in batches, turning regularly, until golden and cooked through. Wipe the pan clean after cooking each batch to remove any breadcrumbs and replenish the oil. Drain the polpette on kitchen towel and serve warm or at room temperature with the simple tomato salsa.

MAKES ABOUT 25

FRICO

{ POTATO AND CHEESE PANCAKE }

2 TEASPOONS OLIVE OIL

½ ONION (ABOUT 100 G/3½ OZ), THINLY
SLICED INTO RINGS

2 SMALL POTATOES (ABOUT 200 G/7 OZ),
PEELED AND CUT INTO SMALL DICE OR
COARSLEY GRATED

150 G (5½ OZ) MONTASIO CHEESE, GRATED

Frico is a bit like a cheesy potato tortilla, but without any eggs. It is eaten in Friuli, a mountainous region in the north-east corner of Italy. It is typically made with Montasio, a cow's milk cheese that is found in Friuli-Venezia Giulia and the Veneto regions. If you cannot find Montasio, look for Piave, Asiago (semi-stagionato) or Latteria. Frico can be eaten on its own, accompanied by a glass red wine, or with polenta. You will need a small non-stick frying pan with a lid to make this dish.

Heat the oil in a saucepan over low heat, then add the onion and potato. Cook, stirring occasionally, for about 20 minutes until the potato is tender and the onion is starting to colour. Add the cheese and stir it in slowly to melt. Remove from the heat and place in a small non-stick frying pan, flattening it so it resembles a thick pancake.

Place the pan over a low heat and cook, covered, for about 10 minutes, until the underside of the 'pancake' is starting to brown and crisp. Use a large plate to help you flip the frico over, and then slide it back into the frying pan. Cook for a further 10 minutes or until the underside is crisp. Slide onto a plate, allow to cool slightly, then cut into wedges and serve warm.

SERVES 4 AS AN APPETISER

SCAGLIOZZI

{ POLENTA CHIPS }

15 G (½ OZ) UNSALTED BUTTER

1 TEASPOON SALT

LOTS OF FRESHLY GROUND BLACK PEPPER

180 G (6½ OZ) INSTANT POLENTA (CORNMEAL)

SEA SALT FLAKES

GARLIC MAYONNAISE (PAGE 257). TO SERVE (OPTIONAL)

A lot of Italian street food originated from the need to make food stretch as far as possible, combining what few ingredients were available with leftovers. This is one such dish. Scagliozzi (pronounced skah-lee-oh-tsee) are fried shapes of leftover polenta, found predominantly in Bari and Naples in the south of Italy. We now see them in restaurants sold as 'polenta chips', and they may be made with stock, herbs or other flavours, but these are the simple version, the street food version of Naples, where they use lots of black pepper. You can bake them in the oven (which makes them healthier) and although not traditional, serve them with a garlic mayonnaise (page 257) as a dipping sauce on the side.

Bring 750 ml (25½ fl oz/3 cups) water to the boil in a medium-sized saucepan, then lower the heat to a steady simmer. Add the butter, salt and pepper and stir to dissolve. When the water returns to a simmer, pour in the polenta in a slow, steady stream stirring the whole time. Keep stirring for 3–4 minutes until the polenta is thick and difficult to stir.

Line a large baking tray with baking paper, then pour over the polenta and spread until it is about 1 cm (½ in) thick. (You can cover the surface with more baking paper and flatten further with a rolling pin, if needed.) Set aside the polenta to harden for at least 12 hours (even a few days is fine). You can put the polenta slab in the fridge but this is only necessary if you live in a warm climate.

Preheat the oven to 210°C (410°F). Line a large baking tray with baking paper.

Cut the cold polenta into 1 cm x 8 cm (½ in x 3¼ in) batons and transfer to the baking tray. Drizzle over a little olive oil and bake for about 30 minutes until golden. Start checking after 20 minutes to make sure they do not crisp up too much.

Eat warm, scattered with sea salt flakes and with garlic mayonnaise for dipping, if desired.

SERVES 4 AS A SIDE DISH

ZEPPOLE con ACCIUGHE e OLIVE

{ ZEPPOLE WITH ANCHOVIES AND OLIVES }

250 G (9 OZ) MEDIUM DESIREE POTATOES

200 G (7 OZ/1⅓ CUPS) PLAIN (ALL-PURPOSE) FLOUR

2 TEASPOONS EXTRA-VIRGIN OLIVE OIL

3 G (⅛ OZ) INSTANT DRIED YEAST

½ TEASPOON SALT

6 ANCHOVY FILLETS

6 LARGE GREEN OLIVES, PITTED

GRAPESEED, PEANUT OR SUNFLOWER OIL, FOR FRYING

Zeppole are traditionally eaten at Christmas time in Calabria, but are so delicious they should be (and often are) eaten at any time of the year. This recipe includes potato in the dough, making them tender and rather addictive. They are stuffed with an anchovy or a green olive, but you can use a firm cheese (such as provolone), nduja (amazingly tasty spreadable Calabrian salami) or cubes of mortadella.

Place the whole unpeeled potatoes in a saucepan of cold water and bring to the boil. Cook for about 30 minutes or until tender when pierced with a fork. Drain, peel and mash or put through a potato ricer (you should have about 200 g/7 oz mashed potato). Keep warm.

Tip the flour onto a clean work surface and make a well in the centre. Place the warm mashed potato in the centre, add the oil and yeast, then bring the ingredients together with your hands to make a smooth dough. Knead for about 5 minutes, then add the salt and work the dough for a further 5 minutes. The dough should be smooth and elastic. Transfer to a lightly oiled bowl, cover with plastic wrap and set aside in a warm draught-free spot for 2 hours or until doubled in size.

Divide the dough into 12 equal-sized pieces. Roll a piece of dough into a ball and flatten slightly with the palm of your hand and make a small indentation. Place an anchovy fillet or an olive in the centre. Close the dough over and roll into a ball. Repeat with the remaining dough, alternating between olives and anchovies. Cover with a clean tea towel and set aside in a warm draught-free spot for 2 hours.

Heat 4–5 cm (1½–2 in) oil in a heavy-based saucepan (or use a deep-fryer) to 180°C (350°F). Test the temperature of the oil by dropping in a cube of bread. If it starts to turn golden in 5 seconds, the oil is ready. Fry the zeppole, 2–4 at a time (depending on the size of your pan), for 3–4 minutes until golden brown, turning regularly to ensure that they cook evenly. Drain on kitchen towel and repeat with the remaining zeppole. Eat while hot for a substantial appetiser.

MAKES 12

PANELLE

{ CHICKPEA FRITTERS }

250 G (9 OZ) CHICKPEA FLOUR (BESAN)

2–3 TABLESPOONS FINELY CHOPPED PARSLEY

GRAPESEED, PEANUT OR SUNFLOWER OIL, FOR FRYING

LEMON WEDGES, TO SERVE

Panelle are said to be a legacy of the Arabic occupancy of Sicily and they are still a very popular street food in Palermo. They are made with chickpea flour, first cooked with water in a similar way to polenta, and then deep-fried. Panelle make great appetisers on their own with only a squeeze of lemon, and they are suitable for those with gluten intolerance, but if you want to eat them like the locals do, make sure they are well salted, and eaten warm in a soft white bread roll.

Place the chickpea flour in a large bowl and whisk to remove any lumps. Slowly pour in 750 ml (25½ fl oz/3 cups) water, whisking as you go, to obtain a smooth batter without lumps. Season with salt and pepper and transfer to a saucepan over low–medium heat, stirring continuously with a wooden spoon. When the mixture starts to thicken, reduce the heat to low. Continue to stir for about 15 minutes, until the mixture is very thick. If there are any lumps, swap the wooden spoon for an electric whisk. Stir in the chopped parsley then remove from the heat.

Working quickly, pour the mixture into a small loaf (bar) tin. Pat it down, cover with plastic wrap and set aside for a few hours, or overnight, to cool completely. Slice the loaf into 2–3 mm (⅛ in) slices and then into triangles.

Heat 2–3 cm (¾–1¼ in) oil in a heavy-based saucepan (or use a deep-fryer) to 180°C (350°F). Test the temperature of the oil by dropping in a scrap of dough. If the dough bubbles and sizzles immediately, the oil is ready. Fry the panelle 3–4 at a time (depending on the size of your pan), for about 2 minutes until they are deep golden all over. The panelle should be slightly crisp on the outside and soft on the inside.

Serve warm, sprinkled with salt and with lemon wedges on the side for squeezing over.

SERVES 8 AS AN APPETISER

MOZZARELLA FRITTA

{ FRIED MOZZARELLA BALLS }

12 (OR MORE, DEPENDING ON THEIR SIZE) SMALL BOCCONCINI

GRAPESEED, PEANUT OR SUNFLOWER OIL, FOR FRYING

SIMPLE TOMATO SALSA (PAGE 261), TO SERVE (OPTIONAL)

CRUMB

PLAIN (ALL-PURPOSE) FLOUR

2 EGGS, LIGHTLY BEATEN WITH A SPLASH OF MILK

HOMEMADE FRESH BREADCRUMBS

Nothing could be simpler or more delicious than fried little balls of cheese. Make sure you drain the bocconcini really well for this recipe; otherwise, the crumbed crust will not stick to the cheese.

Drain the bocconcini for at least 30 minutes, then pat dry with kitchen towel.

Place the flour, egg mixture and breadcrumbs in separate shallow bowls. Lightly roll a bocconcini in the flour, dip in the egg, and then roll in the breadcrumbs. Double-crumb the cheese by dipping in the egg and rolling in the breadcrumbs a second time. The cheese should be completely coated with breadcrumbs so it does not leak out during cooking. Repeat with the remaining bocconcini.

Heat 4–5 cm (1½–2 in) oil in a heavy-based saucepan (or use a deep-fryer) to 180°C (350°F). Test the temperature of the oil by dropping in a cube of bread. If it starts to turn golden in 5 seconds, the oil is ready. Fry the bocconcini for 1–2 minutes, turning frequently, until golden. Drain on kitchen towel and allow to cool a little before serving.

Serve on their own or with the simple tomato salsa for dipping.

SERVES 4

{ PANINI }

Cinque e cinque
Chickpea pancake with eggplant

Panino con fettine impanate e maionnese al limone
Crumbed veal and lemon mayonnaise roll

Panino con tartufata, rucola e parmigiano
Truffled mushrooms, rocket and parmesan roll

Panino con polpettine della nonna
Nonna's little meatballs in a roll

Panino con lesso alla picchiapò
Boiled meat picchiapò-style in a roll

Pizza bianca con mortazza
Roman mortadella sandwich

Cassone verde
Flat bread 'cassone' with greens

There are many English words that have become part of the Italian language in the last 10–20 years. Some have been slightly bastardised or changed, such as the Italian word for jogging, which I just love – *footing*. *Lo snackista* is another such term. It refers to a person who prepares sandwiches and aperitif-style snacks, usually in a bar. I see the snackista as the person who carefully constructs sandwiches, layering delicious ingredients between two pieces of freshly baked bread – I suppose you could also call them a panini maker, but one with a real understanding of the ingredients.

If bread is a staple of the Italian diet, then surely a panino is the best way to eat it. Although the translation of the word panino is sandwich, this is not quite the whole picture. To me, a sandwich is two slices of bread from a rather boxy-looking loaf. A panino, on the other hand, is a crusty bread roll filled with shavings of beef cooked in a piquant tomato-based sauce or a *tartufata* (truffled brown mushrooms) with salty parmigiano cheese. A standard salad and cheese sandwich that you might find in your local sandwich bar is nothing like the creations made by the snackista in Italy.

Today, panini are often eaten at lunchtime in place of the traditional long leisurely lunch that Italians enjoyed before the Westernised continuous workday interrupted their long-standing routine of a long midday break. Panini are the ideal alternative as they often contain hot fillings such as those that I saw on a menu at the Testaccio Market in Rome: homemade meatballs, *lesso alla picchiapò* (boiled meat cooked in a tomato-based sauce), and slices of crumbed veal piled high, often layered with a dose of bitter greens. It feels like something mamma or nonna might make at home.

Florence is another town where lo snackista can be found busily making panini around lunchtime, in one of the many hole-in-the-wall shops. Crowds stand on cobbled streets, eating panini, sipping a small glass of wine (which is the norm among working Italians eating lunch on the street), and having a quick chat with colleagues before heading back to the office. A very civilised and worthy alternative to the long lunch at home.

CINQUE e CINQUE

{ CHICKPEA PANCAKE WITH EGGPLANT }

1 MEDIUM EGGPLANT (AUBERGINE),
CUT INTO 8 SLICES LENGTHWAYS,
ABOUT 3–4 MM (1/4 IN) THICK

1½ TEASPOONS SALT

OLIVE OIL, FOR DRIZZLING

1 GARLIC CLOVE, THINLY SLICED

PINCH OF CHILLI FLAKES

100 G (3½ OZ) CHICKPEA FLOUR (BESAN)

30 ML (1 FL OZ) GRAPESEED OR PEANUT OIL

4 SMALL BAGUETTES OR CIABATTA-STYLE
ROLLS, HALVED

Travelling along the western coast of Italy, at the top of the boot just before it curves towards France, you will find the town of Livorno. There, you can eat cinque e cinque, a savoury pancake made with chickpea flour (called cecina or farinata), served on a French-style baguette with a slice of grilled eggplant (aubergine). Historically, the name stems from five lire (the currency of Italy before entry into the European Union) for the cecina and five lire for the bread. It is served with a splash of olive oil and a good grind of black pepper.

Place the eggplant in a colander over a sink and rub in 1 teaspoon of the salt. Cover with kitchen towel and leave to drain for 1 hour.

Preheat the oven to 200°C (400°F). Pat the eggplant slices dry and transfer to a baking tray. Drizzle over a little olive oil and bake for 10–15 minutes, turning them over halfway and adding a bit more olive oil to the surface of each eggplant slice. Remove from the oven when the edges start to crisp, but the centre of each slice is still tender.

Layer the eggplant slices in a ceramic dish and scatter over the garlic and chilli. Drizzle with a bit more oil and set aside to marinate and soak up the garlic flavour.

Place the chickpea flour in a large bowl and add 300 ml (10 fl oz) water. Whisk for a good 5 minutes to get rid of all the lumps – the mixture will froth up quite a bit. Set aside for 20 minutes or until all the froth floats to the top. Skim the froth from the surface, leaving behind a very liquidy dough. Add 20 ml of the oil and the remaining salt and stir with a wooden spoon.

Preheat your grill (broiler) to high. Coat a cast iron pan with the remaining oil and pour in the liquid dough until it is 1.5–2 mm (⅟₁₆ in) thick. Place under the grill and cook for 7–8 minutes, watching so that it does not burn. The cecina is cooked when it is crisp and golden on top but still soft in the centre.

Cut the cecina into four pieces and place in the baguettes or rolls with a couple of slices of eggplant and a good grinding of black pepper. Ideally, the cecina should still be warm when served.

SERVES 4

PANINO con FETTINE IMPANATE e MAIONNESE al LIMONE

{ CRUMBED VEAL AND LEMON MAYONNAISE ROLL }

400 G (14 OZ) VEAL, CUT INTO 4 SLICES

GRAPESEED OR PEANUT OIL, FOR SHALLOW-FRYING

4 BREAD ROLLS, SUCH AS ROSETTA (PAGE 180), HALVED

LEMON MAYONNAISE (PAGE 256), TO SERVE

HANDFUL ROCKET (ARUGULA) LEAVES, TO SERVE

CRUMB

HOMEMADE FRESH BREADCRUMBS

GOOD PINCH OF FRESHLY GRATED NUTMEG

30 G (1 OZ) PARMESAN CHEESE, FINELY GRATED

PLAIN (ALL-PURPOSE) FLOUR

2 EGGS, BEATEN WITH 1 TABLESPOON MILK

Crumbed veal is a classic that lends itself easily to being stuffed into a roll or a sandwich. I love adding a bit of parmesan to the crumb, so the thinly sliced meat has a delicious, slightly cheesy crust. Pair it with some lemony mayonnaise and a few salad greens to make a panino fit for a king. You could also replace the veal with yearling beef or even with pork if veal is unavailable.

Place the slices of veal one at a time between two pieces of baking paper. Using a meat mallet, bash the veal until it is 2 mm (⅛ in) thick. You can also ask your butcher to do this.

Combine the breadcrumbs, nutmeg and parmesan in a shallow dish. Place the flour and egg wash in separate bowls. Working with one slice of veal at a time, coat in the flour, shaking off the excess, dip in the egg mixture, letting the excess drip back into the bowl and then coat with the breadcrumbs. Make sure that each slice is evenly coated during each of the three stages.

Heat 5 mm (¼ in) of oil in a large frying pan over medium heat. Drop in as many veal slices that will fit in a single layer in the pan. Cook for a few minutes until golden, shaking the pan occasionally so that a bit of oil swirls over the top of the meat, then flip the veal over and cook on the other side. Transfer to a plate and pat dry with kitchen towel.

Cut the veal slices in half and serve in a bread roll with a smear of lemon mayonnaise and a few rocket leaves.

SERVES 4

PANINO con TARTUFATA, RUCOLA e PARMIGIANO

{ TRUFFLED MUSHROOMS, ROCKET AND PARMESAN ROLL }

1 TABLESPOON EXTRA-VIRGIN OLIVE OIL

1 LARGE ANCHOVY

75 G (2¾ OZ) SWISS BROWN MUSHROOMS, FINELY DICED

1 TABLESPOON DRY WHITE WINE

1 LARGE KALAMATA OLIVE, PITTED AND FINELY DICED

2–3 TEASPOONS BLACK TRUFFLE OIL

4 BREAD ROLLS, SUCH AS ROSETTA (PAGE 180), HALVED

THINLY SLICED PARMESAN CHEESE, TO SERVE

HANDFUL ROCKET (ARUGULA) LEAVES, TO SERVE

EXTRA-VIRGIN OLIVE OIL (OPTIONAL)

The combination of truffles, peppery rocket and salty aged cheese is a classic in the paninoteche (sandwich shops) of Florence. Truffles are, however, rather pricey and even truffled mushrooms in a jar (called tartufata) can set you back quite a bit. Black truffle oil however, which can be purchased from good delicatessens and online, is a bit more affordable. Adding this to sautéed brown mushrooms is a rather nice alternative to forking out for the real thing.

Place the olive oil and anchovy in a small frying pan over medium heat and break the anchovy apart with a wooden spoon. Once it becomes fragrant, add the diced mushrooms and warm through. Increase the heat, add the white wine and cook for a couple of minutes until the wine has evaporated. Reduce the heat, add the diced olive and cook for a further 1 minute. Add salt and pepper, to taste.

Remove from the heat and place in a small bowl to cool. Stir through the truffle oil, starting with 2 teaspoons and then taste if it is to your liking. Add another teaspoon, if desired.

Place 1 tablespoon of truffled mushrooms on one side of each roll. Top with a slice of parmesan cheese and a few rocket leaves. Drizzle with extra-virgin olive oil (optional) and top with the other bread half.

SERVES 4

PANINO con POLPETTINE della NONNA

{ NONNA'S LITTLE MEATBALLS IN A ROLL }

25 G (1 OZ) (ABOUT 1 SLICE) WHITE CRUSTLESS BREAD

60 ML (2 FL OZ/¼ CUP) MILK

175 G (6 OZ) MINCED (GROUND) BEEF

75 G (2¾ OZ) MINCED (GROUND) PORK

1 GARLIC CLOVE, MINCED

2 TABLESPOONS ROUGHLY CHOPPED PARSLEY LEAVES

60 G (2 OZ) GRATED PARMESAN CHEESE

PINCH OF FRESHLY GRATED NUTMEG

25 G (1 OZ) GOOD-QUALITY SALAMI, ROUGHLY CHOPPED

1 EGG

2 TABLESPOONS OLIVE OIL

JUICE OF 1 SMALL LEMON

4 BREAD ROLLS, HALVED

HANDFUL ROCKET (ARUGULA) LEAVES

CRUMB

PLAIN (ALL-PURPOSE) FLOUR

1 EGG, LIGHTLY BEATEN WITH A SPLASH OF MILK

HOMEMADE DRIED BREADCRUMBS

Tender and tasty braised meatballs make a wonderful lunch in a bread roll. Crustless white bread soaked in milk ensures that the polpettine stay moist, and the addition of lemon juice in the final few minutes of cooking gives a brilliantly tasty lift to the dish.

Tear the bread into small pieces and soak in the milk for about 10 minutes. Squeeze well and discard the milk.

Place the bread, meat, garlic, parsley, parmesan, nutmeg, salami and egg in a large bowl and season with salt and pepper. Mix well with a spoon or your hands until the mixture is homogenous. Using wet hands, roll golf ball-sized balls and flatten them slightly with the palm of your hand.

Place the flour, egg mixture and breadcrumbs in separate shallow bowls. Coat the meatballs one at a time in the flour, then in the egg and finally in the breadcrumbs. Transfer to a plate, cover with plastic wrap and set aside in the fridge for about 1 hour.

Heat the oil in a frying pan large enough to fit all the meatballs over medium heat. Cook the meatballs until golden brown on one side, then flip over and cook on the other side. Once the meatballs are cooked through, mix the lemon juice with an equal amount of water in a cup and add the liquid to the pan. Cover and cook gently for a further 8–10 minutes.

Place at least two meatballs in each roll and top with fresh peppery rocket and a spoonful of the lovely sauce that the meatballs were cooked in.

SERVES 4

PANINO con LESSO alla PICCHIAPÒ

{ BOILED MEAT PICCHIAPÒ-STYLE IN A ROLL }

2 TABLESPOONS OLIVE OIL

1 WHITE ONION, FINELY CHOPPED

125 ML (4 FL OZ/½ CUP) BEEF STOCK
(PAGE 260)

½ MEDIUM CARROT, THINLY SLICED

400 G (14 OZ) TINNED PEELED TOMATOES

GOOD PINCH OF CHILLI FLAKES

400 G (14 OZ) BOILED BEEF (PAGE 260)

BRANCH OF BASIL LEAVES, PLUS EXTRA
LEAVES, TO SERVE (OPTIONAL)

4 BREAD ROLLS, SUCH AS ROSETTA
(PAGE 180), HALVED

Street food is often about making the most of very little. In Testaccio in Rome, a market stall called Mordi e vai sells bread rolls filled with boiled meat picchiapò-style, in a rich tomato-based sauce with carrots. Cheaper cuts of beef such as those with a lot of tendon and muscle make great meat stock, and Romans have a clever solution as to what can be done with the leftover meat. After having simmered for hours to make stock, it is cut into slices and then re-cooked, by which time it is melt-in-the-mouth tender. Many variations exist of this dish – I have seen Roman mentuccia (mint) used in place of basil, and the meat cut into cubes. Add it to a rosetta roll and you have a rather fine lunch or snack.

Heat the olive oil in a medium-sized saucepan over low heat. Add the onion and cook for 10 minutes until translucent. Add the beef stock and cook for a further 10 minutes until the liquid has reduced by half. Add the carrot and cook for a few minutes, then add the tomatoes and chilli flakes, breaking up the tomatoes with a wooden spoon. Simmer, covered, for about 15 minutes.

Cut the beef into thin slices and remove any obvious pieces of fatty tissue if it is not to your liking. Add the meat to the sauce, together with the branch of basil leaves. Cook for 8–10 minutes until the sauce has soaked through the meat and it is heated through. Add salt and pepper, to taste, and remove the basil.

Divide the meat equally between the bread rolls, making sure that you pick up lots of the lovely sauce as well. Top with basil leaves, if desired.

SERVES 4

PIZZA BIANCA con MORTAZZA

{ ROMAN MORTADELLA SANDWICH }

400 G (14 OZ) STRONG BREAD FLOUR
(SEE PAGE 17), PLUS EXTRA FOR DUSTING

4 G (¼ OZ) INSTANT DRIED YEAST

280 ML (9½ FL OZ) TEPID WATER

2 TABLESPOONS OLIVE OIL

1 TEASPOON SALT

EXTRA-VIRGIN OLIVE OIL

2–3 TABLESPOONS DRIED BREADCRUMBS

SEA SALT, FOR SPRINKLING

24 THIN SLICES MORTADELLA

8 MARINATED ARTICHOKES, DRAINED AND
THINLY SLICED (OPTIONAL)

Romans go crazy for pizza e mortazza, which is nothing more than a sandwich made with plain pizza (pizza bianca), slices of mortadella (called mortazza by the Romans) and a good pinch of salt. In Rome, this is the snack you eat mid-afternoon, and you can even buy it from a food truck of the same name. You need to buy a good-quality Italian mortadella and have it sliced very thinly. I also like to add a couple of pieces of sliced marinated artichokes on top of the mortadella – not traditional but very tasty!

Place the flour in a bowl and whisk in the yeast. Add the water and stir using a wooden spoon, then add the oil and bring the dough together. Transfer to a well-floured work surface, scatter over the salt and knead for about 10 minutes or until the dough is smooth. Alternatively, you can make the dough in a stand mixer with a dough hook attachment. Transfer to a large well-oiled bowl, cover with a clean tea towel and set aside in a warm draught-free spot for at least 2 hours. The dough should more than double in size.

Using oiled hands, transfer the dough to a lightly floured work surface. Punch it down with your hands and knead for about 10 minutes. You can also do this in a stand mixer with a dough hook on low speed. Divide the dough into two, covering the ball you are not working on with a clean tea towel, and knead for a further 5 minutes. Repeat with the other ball of dough. Wet the tea towel, wring it out and cover both balls of dough. Let the dough rest for a further 20 minutes.

Preheat the oven to 210°C (410°F). Grease two large rectangular pizza or baking trays and scatter over the breadcrumbs.

With well-oiled hands, place a ball of dough on your work surface and spread it out with your fingertips to the approximate size of your tray. Transfer to the tray and sprinkle over some sea salt. Repeat with the remaining dough half. Cover with clean tea towels and allow to rest in a draught-free spot for at least another 20 minutes.

Cook one pizza at a time for about 15 minutes, until the edges are golden. Cut each pizza into four and slice through each quarter as if it was pita bread. Place three slices of mortadella and a few artichoke slices (if using) in each and wait a few minutes before serving. The bread should still be warm and the mortadella softened.

SERVES 8

CASSONE VERDE

{ FLAT BREAD 'CASSONE' WITH GREENS }

DOUGH

500 G (1 LB 2 OZ) PLAIN (ALL-PURPOSE) FLOUR

1 TEASPOON SALT

PINCH OF BICARBONATE SODA (BAKING SODA)

200 ML (7 FL OZ) FULL-CREAM (WHOLE) MILK

120 ML (4 FL OZ) OLIVE OIL

FILLING

2 LARGE BUNCHES SPINACH OR OTHER GREENS

4 SPRING ONIONS, WHITE PART ONLY, FINELY CHOPPED

2 TABLESPOONS PARSLEY LEAVES, CHOPPED

½ TEASPOON FRESHLY GRATED NUTMEG

30 G (1 OZ) GRATED PARMESAN CHEESE

Cassone Romagnolo (or Piadina Romagnola) dates back hundreds of years, some say even to Roman times. Traditionally, in the central Italian region of Emilia Romagna, a thin layer of dough made of flour, pork fat, water and salt is rolled out, filled with field herbs, folded in half to form a large pocket and cooked in a pan. There are local variations related to the thickness of the dough and the size of the cassone (more commonly known around the world as piadina) as well as less traditional but other common fillings such as mozzarella and tomato, potato, sausage or pumpkin.

To make the dough, place the flour in a mound on your work surface, scatter over the salt and bicarbonate of soda, then make a small well in the centre of the mound. In a small jug, combine the milk and olive oil, then pour this into the well. Work the liquid into the flour using your fingers, a little at a time, until it all comes together. Work the dough for about 5 minutes, until it is smooth and homogenous. Wrap in plastic wrap and set aside to rest for at least 30 minutes.

Meanwhile, prepare the filling. Bring a large saucepan of salted water to the boil. Trim the roots and stalks from the spinach and discard any wilted or damaged leaves. Thoroughly wash the spinach leaves, rinsing several times to remove any remaining grit and dirt. Plunge in the boiling water and return to the boil. Immediately drain the spinach and refresh in cold water. Squeeze the spinach as hard as you can to remove any excess liquid. You should have about 300 g (10½ oz) cooked spinach. Chop finely, add salt and pepper, to taste, and set aside.

Divide the dough into four equal-sized pieces. Roll out each piece to a 30 cm (12 in) circle, covering each circle with a clean tea towel while you roll out the rest. Divide the filling ingredients evenly among the 'flat breads' placing them on one side of the dough and leaving a 1 cm (½ in) edge. Fold the dough over to form semicircles and push the edges together with your fingers to seal.

Heat a large non-stick frying pan with a lid over medium–high heat. Place one or two cassoni (depending on the size of your pan) in the pan and reduce the heat to low–medium. Cover, and cook for 3–4 minutes on each side, until the dough starts to become golden and crisp. Repeat with the remaining cassoni. Cut each cassone in half and serve with a green salad and a glass of crisp white wine.

MAKES 4

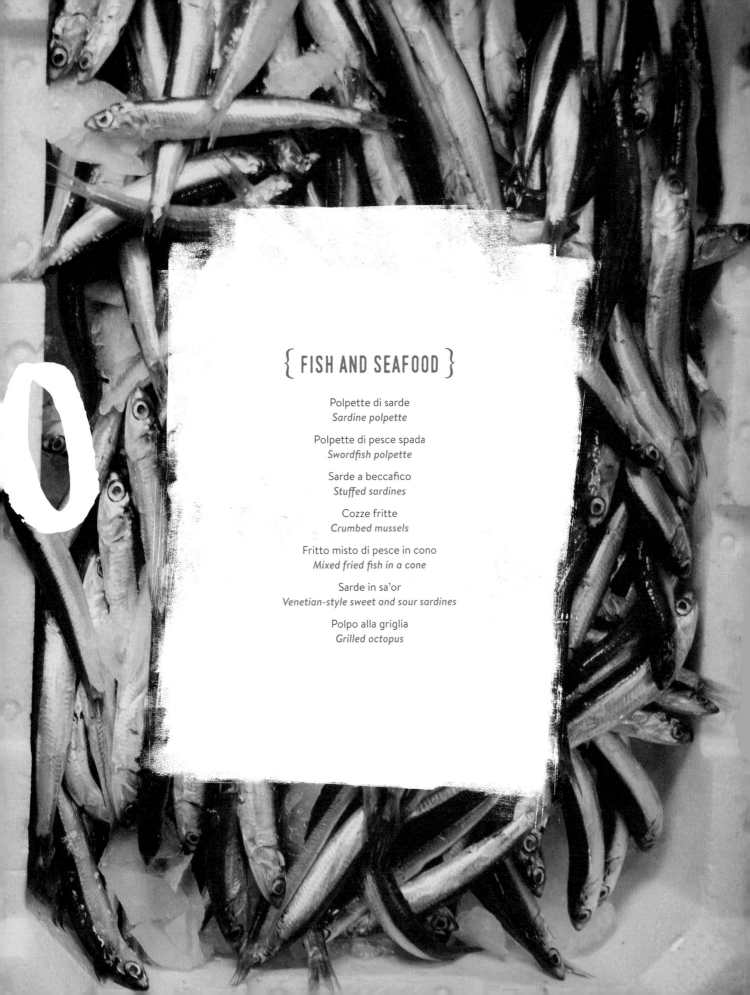

{ FISH AND SEAFOOD }

Polpette di sarde
Sardine polpette

Polpette di pesce spada
Swordfish polpette

Sarde a beccafico
Stuffed sardines

Cozze fritte
Crumbed mussels

Fritto misto di pesce in cono
Mixed fried fish in a cone

Sarde in sa'or
Venetian-style sweet and sour sardines

Polpo alla griglia
Grilled octopus

Italians are spoilt for choice when it comes to fresh seafood, with the Mediterranean Sea to the west, the Adriatic Sea to the east and islands off the southwest coast of the mainland. Even if you live inland, the shore is no more than a couple of hours away, and country towns will have fresh fish markets at least twice a week. Seafood makes a popular street food as it is usually very quick to cook, and smaller bite-sized varieties are very easy to eat without cutlery.

Il poliparo is an old trade from the days when there were very specific roles for street sellers, especially around Venice, the Veneto region and in Palermo in Sicily. Il poliparo was responsible for the preparation of *polipo* (octopus) and other seafood such as sea snails and *canocchie* (a type of crayfish). The octopus is a fascinating creature which, once dunked in boiling water, turns pink and curls up its tentacles. Small octopus can be eaten whole, while the tentacles of larger octopus are often cooked in a delicious light tomato-based sauce until tender and succulent, and scattered with parsley, olive oil, salt and pepper (and garlic if in Sicily).

Although the term poliparo seems to have vanished from common language, boiled octopus is still found in the Vucciria markets in Palermo. Served with a wedge of lemon on the side, it makes a great late night after-party snack. I also found a street seller in the main piazza in Padua serving traditional seafood, in particular octopus, squid and cuttlefish, cooked Veneto-style. He is as close to a poliparo as it gets these days.

Today's fish-based street food can be found throughout Italy — *sarde in sa'or* (sardines in a sweet and sour onion sauce, best eaten several days after they are made) are sold as *cichetti* (snacks) in Venetian bars, often on a round of bread; fried or crumbed fish is often served in paper cones at seaside towns like Rimini, Genoa and Bari, served with an accompanying beer; and bite-sized *beccafico* (stuffed) sardines can be found at the markets in Palermo, Messina and Catania in Sicily.

POLPETTE di SARDE

{ SARDINE POLPETTE }

50 G (1¾ OZ) CRUSTLESS BREAD

125 ML (4 FL OZ/½ CUP) MILK

600 G (1 LB 5 OZ) SARDINES, FILLETED AND CLEANED

50 G (1¾ OZ) PARMESAN, GRATED

1 GARLIC CLOVE, CRUSHED

PINCH OF FRESHLY GRATED NUTMEG

1 TABLESPOON FINELY CHOPPED MINT LEAVES

50 G (1¾ OZ) CURRANTS, SOAKED IN 60 ML (2 FL OZ/¼ CUP) WARM WATER FOR 15 MINUTES AND DRAINED

1 LARGE EGG, LIGHTLY BEATEN

1–2 TABLESPOONS BREADCRUMBS (IF NEEDED)

OLIVE OIL, FOR FRYING

LEMON WEDGES, TO SERVE

GARLIC MAYONNAISE (PAGE 257), TO SERVE (OPTIONAL)

Sardines have always been inexpensive and plentiful and were historically often the seafood of choice for those with little money. And they are delicious! They're easy to fillet, especially if you plan on making meatballs with them; however, you can also buy them ready-filleted if you are short on time or a little on the squeamish side.

Soak the bread in the milk for a couple of minutes, then drain and squeeze out any excess liquid. Transfer to a bowl and set aside.

Wash the sardines well and pat dry with kitchen towel. Finely chop the sardine fillets and remove the skin as it may have a few fine bones attached. Transfer to the bowl with the soaked bread and add the parmesan, garlic, nutmeg, mint, drained currants, egg and salt and pepper, to taste. Add a few breadcrumbs if the mixture appears too wet – you want a firm consistency, so that the polpette don't fall apart when cooking.

Wet your hands with a little water and roll the mixture into golf ball-sized balls, about 20 g (¾ oz) in weight, then flatten slightly.

Place enough olive oil in a frying pan to cover the base. Pan-fry the polpette over a medium heat for about 8 minutes, flipping over halfway, until cooked through and golden brown. Serve as an appetiser with lemon wedges and garlic mayonnaise, if desired.

MAKES ABOUT 35

POLPETTE di PESCE SPADA

{ SWORDFISH POLPETTE }

GRAPESEED OIL OR PEANUT OIL, FOR FRYING

450 G (1 LB) SWORDFISH, CUT INTO 1 CM (½ IN) CUBES

40 G (1¼ OZ) PINE NUTS

1 TEASPOON GROUND CINNAMON

2 TEASPOONS FINELY CHOPPED OREGANO LEAVES

2 TABLESPOONS FINELY CHOPPED FLAT-LEAF PARSLEY LEAVES

50 G (1¾ OZ) GRATED PARMESAN

1 LARGE EGG, LIGHTLY BEATEN

100 G (3½ OZ) BREADCRUMBS

1 TEASPOON ORANGE ZEST

1 TABLESPOON FRESHLY SQUEEZED ORANGE JUICE

30 G (1 OZ) CURRANTS, SOAKED IN 60 ML (2 FL OZ/¼ CUP) WARM WATER FOR 15 MINUTES AND DRAINED (OPTIONAL)

Swordfish is caught in the Strait of Messina, between the island of Sicily and the Calabrian coast. Walking past a fishmonger in the market of Catania, or Syracuse, you will probably see a piece of the whole swordfish (including the sword) on the bench, waiting to be sliced. You can't get much fresher than this. I ate a couple of swordfish polpette walking through the Palermo markets, served in a small container and eaten with a skewer. They were sweet, with a hint of cinnamon and orange. You can substitute another firm-fleshed fish such as marlin or yellowfin kingfish if you cannot find swordfish.

Heat a splash of oil in a medium-sized frying pan over medium heat. Add the swordfish, pine nuts and ground cinnamon and cook for 2–3 minutes, until the fish takes on some colour and is just cooked through. Set aside in a medium-sized bowl to cool to room temperature.

Add the herbs, parmesan, egg, breadcrumbs, orange zest and juice and currants, if using. Season with salt and pepper and mix to combine well. Roll small balls with the mixture, about 30 g (1 oz) in weight, and place on a baking tray. Cover with plastic wrap and set aside in the fridge for at least 1 hour and up to 3–4 hours.

Place enough olive oil in a frying pan to cover the base. Pan-fry the meatballs, turning as required, for 2–3 minutes until pale golden on all sides.

These polpette are equally nice hot, warm or at room temperature with a garden salad on the side.

MAKES APPROXIMATELY 25

SARDE a BECCAFICO

{ STUFFED SARDINES }

24 LARGE SARDINES, FILLETED AND CLEANED, TAILS LEFT INTACT

1 TABLESPOON EXTRA-VIRGIN OLIVE OIL

2 GARLIC CLOVES, FINELY CHOPPED

75 G (2¾ OZ) BREADCRUMBS FROM DAY-OLD BREAD

1 TABLESPOON FINELY CHOPPED FLAT-LEAF PARSLEY LEAVES

30 G (1 OZ) CURRANTS, SOAKED IN 60 ML (2 FL OZ/¼ CUP) WARM WATER AND DRAINED

30 G (1 OZ) PINE NUTS, TOASTED

ZEST AND JUICE OF 1 LEMON PLUS 1 LEMON, SLICED

1½ TABLESPOONS FRESHLY SQUEEZED ORANGE JUICE

2 SMALL ORANGES, HALVED AND SLICED

8 FRESH BAY LEAVES

In Sicily sardines are often cleverly paired with sweet currants, citrus fruits and pine nuts, giving them not only a sweet taste but also an acidic and savoury kick. You don't have to put them on skewers, they can be baked side by side, with alternating slices of citrus fruit and bay leaves. Super-fresh sardines work best for this recipe.

Pat the sardines dry with kitchen towel and set aside.

Heat the oil in a non-stick frying pan over medium heat. Toss in the garlic, breadcrumbs, parsley and a good pinch of salt. Toast for a few minutes until the garlic is fragrant and the breadcrumbs have taken on a bit of colour. Tip the mixture into a small bowl, then add the drained currants, toasted pine nuts, lemon zest and orange juice and give everything a good stir.

Preheat the oven to 160°C (320°F). Soak 8 wooden skewers in cold water for 15 minutes.

Prepare your skewers by threading on a slice of orange. Lay a sardine fillet on a clean work surface and place 1 teaspoon of filling at the widest end. The filling may fall out a bit at the sides if you have smaller sardines, but this is OK. Roll up the fillet and thread onto the skewer. Thread a slice of lemon onto the skewer, then add another rolled-up sardine followed by a bay leaf. Add a final rolled sardine and finish with another slice of orange. Transfer to a baking dish and repeat until you have 8 skewers. Drizzle liberally with olive oil and bake for 20 minutes.

Drizzle the skewers with lemon juice and allow to rest for 10 minutes before serving.

MAKES 8 SKEWERS

COZZE FRITTE

{ CRUMBED MUSSELS }

125 ML (4 FL OZ/½ CUP) WHITE WINE

1 KG (2 LB 3 OZ) LIVE MUSSELS, SCRUBBED AND DEBEARDED, BROKEN SHELLS DISCARDED

75 G (2¾ OZ/½ CUP) PLAIN (ALL-PURPOSE) FLOUR

2 EGGS, LIGHTLY BEATEN WITH A SPLASH OF MILK

125 G (4½ OZ) HOMEMADE FRESH BREADCRUMBS, PLUS EXTRA, IF NEEDED

SUNFLOWER, GRAPESEED OR PEANUT OIL, FOR FRYING

SEA SALT FLAKES

LEMON WEDGES, TO SERVE

The Adriatic coast has some of Italy's freshest shellfish. Mussels are plump, fresh and easy to find at markets. They are particularly meaty and delicious covered in breadcrumbs and fried – something that would not suit smaller, more delicate molluscs. I like giving them two coats of breadcrumbs and serving them in a paper cone with lemon wedges, like they do at the seaside, even at home.

Pour the wine into a large frying pan with a lid, and turn the heat to high. When the wine starts to bubble, tip the mussels in and put the lid on. Shake the pan every minute or so, then start checking for open shells. Remove any open mussels and transfer to a bowl. Keep steaming the remaining mussels with the lid on, shaking the pan and removing the mussels as they open. Discard any shells that are unopened after 5 minutes.

Remove the mussels from their shells and place in a bowl of water. Trim any remaining beards and pat them dry.

Fill three separate shallow dishes with the flour, egg mixture and the breadcrumbs. Roll the mussels lightly in flour, then dip in the egg and roll in the breadcrumbs. If you want to double-crumb your mussels, dip them in the egg and breadcrumbs again. Repeat with the remaining mussels.

Heat enough oil for deep-frying in a large heavy-based saucepan or deep-fryer to 180°C (350°F). Test the temperature of the oil by dropping in a cube of bread. If it turns golden in 5 seconds, the oil is ready. Add the mussels and fry, turning frequently, for 3–4 minutes until golden.

Serve warm as an appetiser, scattered with sea salt flakes and lemon wedges for squeezing over.

SERVES 4

FRITTO MISTO di PESCE in CONO

{ MIXED FRIED FISH IN A CONE }

800 G (1 LB 12 OZ) MIXED SEAFOOD (SUCH AS BABY CALAMARI, WHITEBAIT, SCHOOL PRAWNS/SHRIMP, FLATHEAD TAILS AND SCALLOPS), CUT INTO BITE-SIZED PIECES

GRAPESEED OR PEANUT OIL, FOR FRYING

FINE SEMOLINA, FOR DUSTING

SEA SALT FLAKES

LEMON WEDGES OR LEMON MAYONNAISE (PAGE 256), TO SERVE

Eating freshly caught seafood, just fried and served in a cone on the beach is one of the joys of summer, especially in seaside towns like Rimini. I love serving this dish to friends in the early evening with a refreshing Prosecco. You can use your favourite shellfish, or fish such as mackerel, sardines or flathead, cut into bite-sized pieces. If you ask your fishmonger to fillet and clean the fish for you, this becomes a simple and quick dish. Serve with lemon wedges or, if you have a bit more time, a homemade Lemon mayonnaise.

Wash and pat dry the seafood with kitchen towels, putting the different types of fish into separate small bowls (as they have slightly different cooking times).

Heat enough oil for deep-frying in a large heavy-based saucepan, wok or deep-fryer to 190°C (375°F). Check that your oil is hot enough by dropping in a tiny piece of fish. It should immediately start bubbling.

Working with one type of seafood at a time, dust each piece lightly with semolina. The easiest way to do this is to drop the fish pieces into a large wire-meshed strainer. Sprinkle a tablespoon of semolina over the fish and toss well, catching the excess semolina in a large bowl underneath.

Fry the fish in batches for 1–2 minutes, depending on their size, until golden. Drain on kitchen towel and repeat with the remaining seafood.

Serve the seafood in cones, if desired, scattered with sea salt flakes and lemon wedges or lemon mayonnaise on the side.

SERVES 4

SARDE in SA'OR

{Venetian-style sweet and sour sardines}

125 ML (4 FL OZ/½ CUP) OLIVE OIL

3 MEDIUM ONIONS, THINLY SLICED ON A MANDOLINE

5 BLACK PEPPERCORNS, LIGHTLY CRUSHED, PLUS EXTRA, IF DESIRED

1 FRESH BAY LEAF

125 ML (4 FL OZ/½ CUP) WHITE WINE VINEGAR

20 SARDINES, FILLETED AND CLEANED

PLAIN (ALL PURPOSE) FLOUR, FOR DUSTING

SEA SALT FLAKES

2 TABLESPOONS SULTANAS (GOLDEN RAISINS)

2 TABLESPOONS PINE NUTS, LIGHTLY TOASTED

EXTRA-VIRGIN OLIVE OIL, FOR DRIZZLING

SMALL HANDFUL PARSLEY LEAVES, CHOPPED, FOR GARNISH (OPTIONAL)

I have eaten these sardines since I was a child. Mamma would keep a ceramic container in the fridge with layers of sardines and soft sweet onions, and my sister and I would sneak a couple in the evening after everyone had gone to bed.

Heat half of the olive oil in a large non-stick frying pan over a low–medium heat. Add the onion, peppercorns and bay leaf and cook, stirring frequently, for about 20 minutes or until the onion is soft and lightly golden. Add a little water if the onion is browning too quickly. Add the vinegar and cook for a further 10 minutes, ensuring that the onion remains moist. Transfer to a bowl and set aside.

Pat dry the sardines with kitchen towel, then dust lightly with flour on both sides. Heat the remaining olive oil in the same frying pan and cook the sardines over a medium heat for about 2 minutes on each side until golden. Drain on kitchen towel to soak up any excess oil and sprinkle with sea salt flakes.

In a ceramic container, preferably with its own lid, place a layer of cooked onion. Scatter over a few sultanas and pine nuts (and a few more black peppercorns if you like), then add a layer of cooked sardines. Repeat the layers 3–4 times, finishing with a layer of onion. Drizzle over a little extra-virgin olive oil if the mixture looks dry and garnish with a few chopped parsley leaves, if desired.

Set aside in the fridge, covered, for at least 1–2 days before serving. The sardines will keep for up to 1 week.

SERVES 4

POLPO *alla* GRIGLIA

{ GRILLED OCTOPUS }

800 G (1 LB 12 OZ) OCTOPUS (ABOUT 1 MEDIUM-SIZED OCTOPUS)

EXTRA-VIRGIN OLIVE OIL

HANDFUL PARSLEY LEAVES, CHOPPED

SEA SALT FLAKES

LEMON WEDGES, TO SERVE

Octopus and squid are found all around the Venetian lagoon and in the town of Padova, not too far from Venice, there is a street food stall that only sells seafood. Grilled, stuffed and fried, it offers all sorts of traditional fish that you eat with a toothpick while standing in the Piazza della Frutta in the centre of town, drinking a glass of Prosecco.

Prepare the octopus by removing the tentacles just below the eyes. You can also use the head if you like, but cleaning it can be a bit messy so it's best to ask your fishmonger to do this. Wash the tentacles under plenty of cold water. You do not need to remove the skin from the octopus.

Bring a large saucepan of water to the boil and submerge the octopus for 10 seconds. Lift the octopus out of the water (the legs will have curled up) and submerge again for a further 10 seconds. Repeat this process 3–4 times as it helps to tenderise the flesh. Return the octopus to the boiling water and cook, covered, for 15 minutes. Remove the pan from the heat and set aside, allowing the octopus to rest in the water until the water cools completely.

Remove the octopus and cut into 7.5 cm (3 in) pieces. Heat a chargrill pan or barbecue to high. Rub a little olive oil on the octopus and grill or barbecue for about 4 minutes, turning frequently, until evenly cooked through.

Serve the octopus warm or cold, scattered with chopped parsley, sea salt flakes and lemon wedges for squeezing over.

SERVES 4

iL PORCHETTA

{ MEAT }

Polpettine di bar
Fried meatballs

Panino con porchetta
Porchetta roll

Olive all'ascolana
Stuffed fried olives

Gnocchi fritti
Fried 'gnocchi' bread

Arrosticini
Grilled lamb bites

Bombette Pugliesi
Little meat bombs from Puglia

Luganega con aceto
Pork sausage bites

Traditionally, the *porchettaio* (porchetta-maker) was a specialist
in preparing *porchetta* (roast pork), a rustic dish originating in
central Italy. However, if you look up the word porchettaio in
the Italian dictionary you may have trouble finding it, as it is no
longer used very often. The word may have gone out of fashion,
but porchetta vans that sell slices of roasted pork belly, or more
traditionally, entire deboned pigs, have not. The vans can be found
at markets, *sagre* (fairs) and even concerts in some regions, but
especially in Lazio, Umbria, Tuscany and Abruzzo, where it has
been made for centuries.

When the entire pig is prepared, the body is deboned, stuffed
and carefully rolled so that a good layer of skin and fat protects
the inner meat and stuffing while it is being cooked, usually in an
oven but traditionally over an open-wood fire. The stuffing varies
from region to region and can include liver, lard, rosemary, garlic,
wild fennel, dill or pepper. Ideally, the crust should be crisp on the
outside, the rolled meat tender, and the stuffing fragrantly salty.

Although I had seen porchetta vans in the piazzas in Spoleto
and Florence, I unexpectedly found one along a suburban road

when I was travelling through the town of Pescara in Abruzzo. Evening had set in and I was walking back to my accommodation, along a different route that I had taken earlier that day. I spied a well-lit van in the distance with signs advertising *porchetta cotta al mattone* (roast pork belly cooked on a brick), *polli allo spiedo* (roast chicken) and *carni nostrane* (traditional meats from the region), plus a cartoon-like illustration of a pig all rolled up and roasted on the front of the van. I started chatting to the porchettaio, a jolly and generous fellow who told me a bit about the van and his products. He gave me a taste of the porchetta (which was succulent, tender and rosemary-scented) and told me that the pigs used were local and that although trade was slower in winter, he would still sell to older folk, who would buy their dinner to take back to their apartments. As if on cue, an older gentleman came along and ordered €5 of porchetta and a serve of roasted vegetables as a side. They were all packed carefully in a foil container, sealed and handed over with plastic cutlery and a napkin. Clearly dinner was sorted – cheap, delicious and most importantly, traditional, made by an artisan and local.

POLPETTINE di BAR

{FRIED MEATBALLS}

150 G (5½ OZ) (1 MEDIUM) POTATO

30 G (1 OZ) CRUSTLESS BREAD

80 ML (2½ FL OZ/⅓ CUP) MILK

250 G (9 OZ) MINCED (GROUND) BEEF

1 EGG

2 TABLESPOONS CHOPPED FLAT-LEAF
PARSLEY LEAVES

1 GARLIC CLOVE, CRUSHED

½ TEASPOON SEA SALT FLAKES, PLUS EXTRA,
TO SERVE

½ TEASPOON PEPPER, FRESHLY GROUND

40 G (1¼ OZ) GRATED PARMESAN

GRAPESEED, PEANUT OR SUNFLOWER OIL,
FOR SHALLOW-FRYING

CRUMB

PLAIN (ALL-PURPOSE) FLOUR,

1 EGG, LIGHTLY BEATEN WITH A SPLASH
OF MILK

HOMEMADE FRESH BREADCRUMBS

Growing up, we usually ate meatballs in a sauce accompanied by pasta, potato mash or polenta, but these polpettine also make great bar food. During a recent trip to Venice, a restaurant and bar called La Vedova was recommended to me not only through foodie connections on social media but also through my host Flavia, who is friends with the owner. I was told to try the fried meat polpettine, as 'they sell them more quickly than they can make them'. So, traipsing along the laneways one evening near Ca D'Oro, I found La Vedova. I stood behind a long line of people at the bar, waiting for a polpettina and a glass of Prosecco. It was absolutely worth the wait – just-fried meatballs, crunchy on the outside and so tasty on the inside, served in a tiny serviette and eaten in just a couple of bites.

Place the whole potato in a saucepan of cold water, cover and bring to the boil. Cook for about 30 minutes until tender. Drain, peel and mash or push through a potato ricer. Set aside to cool.

Soak the bread in the milk for 5 minutes, then drain and squeeze the bread to remove the excess liquid. Transfer to a large bowl.

Add the potato and the remaining ingredients except the oil to the large bowl. Combine the ingredients with a large wooden spoon or your hands until the mixture comes together.

Roll the mixture into small balls, about 20 g (¾ oz) each.

To crumb the meatballs, fill three separate shallow dishes with the flour, egg mixture and breadcrumbs. Dredge the meatballs one at a time in the flour, then the egg and finally the breadcrumbs. Set aside on a plate.

Heat about 1 cm (½ in) of oil in a large heavy-based saucepan over a medium heat. Fry the meatballs in batches for about 3 minutes, turning until they are evenly cooked and deep brown.

Drain the meatballs on kitchen towel and serve warm, scattered with extra salt flakes.

MAKES ABOUT 20

PANINO con PORCHETTA

{ PORCHETTA ROLL }

8 LARGE GARLIC CLOVES, MINCED

1½ TABLESPOONS ROSEMARY LEAVES, FINELY CHOPPED

1½ TABLESPOONS WILD FENNEL OR FENNEL FRONDS, FINELY CHOPPED

2 HEAPED TABLESPOONS SEA SALT FLAKES, PLUS EXTRA TO SERVE

1 TABLESPOON OLIVE OIL

3 KG (6 LB 10 OZ) PORK BELLY, LOIN ATTACHED, SKIN ON

BREAD ROLLS, TO SERVE

Porchetta is one of the ultimate street foods of central Italy. When making it at home, use a piece of pork belly with the loin still attached and the skin on. If the loin has been separated, you can purchase a piece of loin and stuff this into the middle of the belly. This recipe is from my friend Verdiana's sister who lives in Spoleto. This recipe makes enough porchetta to feed a group of 12 hungry friends or family with leftovers for a few days.

In a small bowl, make a paste with the garlic, rosemary, fennel, salt and olive oil.

Score the flesh side of the pork and rub the paste into the flesh with your finger tips. Roll up tightly and tie with kitchen string at 6 cm (2½ in) intervals. Place the rolled porchetta on a wire rack in a roasting tin, and set aside in the fridge, uncovered, to rest overnight (your fridge will have a divine smell of garlic).

Remove the pork from the fridge and pat dry with kitchen towel if the skin is at all damp. Allow the pork to come to room temperature for 1 hour before cooking.

Preheat the oven to 160°C (320°F).

Cook the porchetta for 3½ hours. At the end of cooking, turn up the heat to 250°C (480°F) (or as high as your oven will go) for about 30 minutes, turning the porchetta regularly and checking that it doesn't burn. This last step ensures that a crackling forms on the outside of the porchetta. Remove from the oven and set aside to rest, uncovered, for at least 30 minutes.

Cut the bread rolls in half and thinly slice the porchetta. Pile the porchetta onto the bottom half of each roll making sure you include thin pieces of crackling. Sprinkle with sea salt and serve.

OLIVE ALL'ASCOLANA

{ STUFFED FRIED OLIVES }

OLIVE OIL, FOR COOKING

25 G (1 OZ) FINELY DICED CARROT

25 G (1 OZ) FINELY DICED CELERY

25 G (1 OZ) FINELY CHOPPED ONION

75 G (2¾ OZ) MINCED (GROUND) BEEF

75 G (2¾ OZ) MINCED (GROUND) PORK

75 G (2¾ OZ) MINCED (GROUND) CHICKEN

60 ML (2 FL OZ/¼ CUP) DRY WHITE WINE

PINCH OF FRESHLY GRATED NUTMEG

PINCH OF GROUND CLOVES

20 G (¾ OZ) GRATED PARMESAN

¼ TEASPOON LEMON ZEST

10 G (⅓ OZ) CRUSTLESS BREAD, TORN INTO CHUNKS

1 SMALL EGG, LIGHTLY BEATEN

50 LARGE GREEN OLIVES

GARLIC MAYONNAISE (PAGE 257) (OPTIONAL)

CRUMB

PLAIN (ALL PURPOSE) FLOUR

1 EGG, LIGHTLY BEATEN WITH A SPLASH OF MILK

HOMEMADE FRESH BREADCRUMBS

In the region of Le Marche you will find these little savoury bites for sale at food trucks – they are salty, fried and highly addictive. To be authentic, they should be made with a local variety of large green olives in brine called Tenere Ascolane. If you can't find these, don't worry, it's fine to use other large green olives. They are stuffed with three kinds of meat, rolled in breadcrumbs and then fried. They require a bit of work, and ideally an olive pitter but they're very impressive for when guests drop by!

Heat a good glug of olive oil in a frying pan over a low–medium heat. Add the carrot, celery and onion and cook, stirring occasionally, for about 10 minutes until soft but not coloured. Add the mince and cook for a few minutes, stirring frequently, until the meat is browned. Turn up the heat and pour in the wine. Stir frequently until the wine evaporates, then transfer the mixture to a bowl and set aside to cool.

Place the cooled mixture in a food processor and add the nutmeg, ground clove, parmesan, lemon zest, bread and egg. Pulse a few times until a paste forms. Transfer to a small bowl and set aside in the fridge, covered, until ready to use.

To prepare the olives, remove the pit with an olive pitter and then, starting at the end where the stalk was attached, cut a spiral with a paring knife through the olive from the top to the base, so that it can be opened up and the filling put inside. Repeat with the remaining olives.

Make small olive-pit shapes with the filling and insert them in the space left behind by the olive pit, then close the spiral. The olives should be only slightly bigger than before the pit was removed.

To crumb the olives, fill three separate shallow dishes with the flour, egg wash and breadcrumbs. Dredge the olives one at a time, first in the flour, then in the egg and finally the breadcrumbs. If you like, double-crumb the olives to get a thicker coating. Set aside on a plate.

Heat plenty of olive oil in a small saucepan to 180°C (350°F). Deep-fry the olives until golden all over – this will take less than 1 minute. Drain on kitchen towel and serve warm with garlic mayonnaise, if desired.

MAKES 50 FRIED OLIVES

GNOCCHI FRITTI

{ FRIED 'GNOCCHI' BREAD }

300 G (10½ OZ) PLAIN (ALL-PURPOSE) FLOUR

30 G (1 OZ) COLD UNSALTED BUTTER, DICED

2 TEASPOONS INSTANT DRIED YEAST

150 ML (5 FL OZ) TEPID WATER

1 SCANT TEASPOON SALT

GRAPESEED, PEANUT OR SUNFLOWER OIL,
FOR FRYING

SLICED PROSCIUTTO OR SALAME, TO SERVE

When I first saw a sign for gnocchi fritti in Bologna, I thought it meant fried potato gnocchi, so I went in and asked. When I saw them in the display cabinet, they looked like thin pieces of rectangular dough, slightly puffed, and with slices of various salumi between them. The shopkeeper explained that they were used as bread and fried. And (to my surprise), they did not contain potatoes. I love all the regional differences in terminology! When in doubt, always ask a local. Traditionally, these contain strutto (pork fat) and are deep-fried in it as well, although I have used butter and oil respectively as substitutes.

Tip the flour onto a clean work surface and make a little well in the centre. Place the butter in the well and work it into the flour with your fingers. Sprinkle over the yeast and pour in the water, a little at a time, incorporating it as you go. Finally, sprinkle over the salt and combine well. Knead the dough for 10 minutes, by which time it should be smooth, soft and elastic. Alternatively, you can make the dough using a stand mixer with a dough hook attachment on low speed.

Transfer the dough to a medium-sized bowl, cover with plastic wrap and set aside to rest in a warm draught-free place for 2 hours, or until doubled in sized.

Place the dough on a lightly floured work surface and roll out to a 3–4 mm (¼ in) thick rectangle. Using a fluted pastry cutter, cut out 8 cm x 10 cm (3¼ in x 4 in) rectangles. You can also cut triangles or diamonds if you like.

Heat 3–4 cm (1¼–1½ in) of oil in a heavy-based saucepan (or use a deep-fryer) to 190°C (375°F). Test the heat of the oil by dropping in some pastry scraps. If they sizzle straightaway, the oil is ready. Carefully drop in 1–2 'gnocchi' (depending on the size of your pan). They will take 30–40 seconds to cook on each side and will puff up quite a bit. When one side is golden, flip over and cook the other side.

Drain on kitchen towel and eat warm or cool, served with slices of prosciutto or salame. You can even fold the 'gnocchi' over onto themselves like a sandwich.

These are best eaten on the day they are made.

MAKES 15–20

TRATTORIA

IL BARGELLO

ARROSTICINI

{ GRILLED LAMB BITES }

500 G (1 LB 2 OZ) BONELESS LAMB SHOULDER, CUT INTO 3/4 CM (1/3 IN) DICE
GOOD-QUALITY EXTRA-VIRGIN OLIVE OIL
SEA SALT FLAKES
CHILLI FLAKES
CRUSTY BREAD, TO SERVE

Tradition has it that arrosticini were eaten by shepherds while they were in the hills of Abruzzo tending their sheep. They didn't need much to make a fine meal – tiny cubes of marbled mutton, salt, skewers and an open fire. The arrosticini you find in osterie, bars and food vans haven't changed much since those times, except they are now often cooked on a long wood charcoal grill that turns the skewers slowly and evenly. Herbs such as rosemary or sage can be placed over the coals for flavour and a good balance of fat and lean meat is essential. If you want to be authentic, remember to eat the meat directly from the skewer, not with a fork. You can use a barbecue with woodchips at home or even a grill (broiler) at high heat, just make sure you turn them frequently and only cook until the meat is just cooked through.

If using bamboo skewers, soak them in cold water for 30 minutes to prevent them burning.

Preheat a barbecue or grill (broiler) to high.

Thread the diced lamb onto the skewers, sprinkle over plenty of pepper and a splash of olive oil, then place on the barbecue or grill and cook, turning frequently, for about 5 minutes or until just cooked through.

Sprinkle with sea salt and chilli flakes and drizzle over a little olive oil. Serve with crusty bread on the side. Paired with a salad, this makes a lovely light meal.

MAKES 8 SKEWERS

BOMBETTE PUGLIESI

{LITTLE MEAT BOMBS FROM PUGLIA}

500 G (1 LB 2 OZ) PORK NECK OR SHOULDER, CUT INTO 24 THIN STEAKS

150 G (5½ OZ) MILD PANCETTA, THINLY SLICED

100 G (3½ OZ) PECORINO SARDO, SLICED

HANDFUL PARSLEY LEAVES

EXTRA-VIRGIN OLIVE OIL, FOR BRUSHING

If you find yourself at a street food event in southern Puglia, you will probably find bombette, or 'little bombs', so called because of their typical shape. Layers of thinly sliced marbled pork neck are stuffed with a piece of medium-aged sheep's milk cheese (typically canestrato Pugliese but you can use a pecorino sardo or caciocavallo), skewered and roasted over hot coals. They can also be baked in the oven and put under a hot grill for a few minutes. They are great served with beer; a game of Italian cards wouldn't go astray either!

Preheat the oven to 200°C (400°F). Soak four wooden skewers in cold water for 30 minutes.

Using the flat side of a hand-held meat tenderiser, pound the pork steaks until they are 2–3 mm (⅛ in) thick. Cut into 10 cm x 15 cm (4 in x 6 in) rectangles and season with salt and pepper. Place a slice of pancetta, a slice of cheese and a few parsley leaves on each rectangle of pork, then roll up and secure with a toothpick. Repeat with the remaining ingredients.

Preheat a grill (broiler) or barbecue to high.

Thread six bombette onto a wooden skewer and brush lightly with olive oil. Bake for about 15 minutes, turning every 5 minutes so the bombette cook evenly, and brushing with a bit more olive oil if they look dry. Transfer to a grill or barbecue and cook briefly to slightly char the bombette.

Remove the bombette from the skewers and serve.

MAKES 24

LUGANEGA con ACETO

{ PORK SAUSAGE BITES }

SPLASH OF OLIVE OIL

4 GOOD-QUALITY PLAIN PORK SAUSAGES,
CUT INTO BITE-SIZED PIECES

2 TABLESPOONS RED WINE VINEGAR

2 TABLESPOONS BALSAMIC VINEGAR

Several of my extended family live in Friuli-Venezia Giulia. On my last visit, I was telling my cousin Edda about this book. She suggested I include one of her favourite street snacks – luganega con aceto. Luganega is a regional word meaning sausage, usually pork. In this dish, the sausage is pan-fried and vinegar is added towards the end of cooking. The sour vinegar complements the fatty pork perfectly and bite-sized pieces of sausage can be eaten with skewers or toothpicks. In Friuli this dish is often served with polenta.

Heat the olive oil in a frying pan over medium heat. Add the sausage and cook, covered, for about 10 minutes until the cooked through. Check the sausage every few minutes and turn occasionally so they cook evenly.

Place the vinegars in a bowl and stir so they are evenly mixed. Once the sausages are cooked through, turn up the heat and add the combined vinegars, cooking for a couple of minutes until a little liquid evaporates. Toss the sausage pieces so they are well covered with the liquid and serve with toothpicks and a glass of red wine.

{ BREADS AND BAKED GOODS }

Focaccia Barese
Focaccia Bari-style

Calzone con cipolla e olive
Onion and olive calzone

Fiadoni Abruzzesi
Puffed cheese bites

Taralli Napoletani
Neapolitan taralli

Crescentine
Pan-cooked flat bread

Rustico Leccese
Rustico pastry

Tarallini Pugliesi
Little taralli from Puglia

Rosette di pane
Rosetta bread rolls

Pan di ramerino
Rosemary buns

Bread is central to every Italian meal. Depending on exactly where in Italy you are, *grissini* (bread sticks), slices of fresh bread or *crescentine* (a small flattened bread cooked over fire in a terracotta tigella and a specialty of central Italy) will be served to you before the start of a meal. In fact, a meal would be almost incomplete without some sort of bread on the table. My mother's brother Fidenzio was such a bread fiend that if he was eating out at a restaurant, my aunt would bring a couple of bread rolls in her handbag – just in case they didn't provide enough bread for his needs. Every time he ate, it was a mouthful of bread to a mouthful of food.

The ancient trade of fornaio dates back to Roman times when there were over 400 government-controlled public ovens in Rome. At this time, bread was made without yeast and used *farro* (spelt) as a grain. By the Middle Ages, oil, butter, aromatic herbs, dried fruit and spices had been added to many bread recipes, so that a large variety of savoury and sweet yeasted breads were available. Many of those older traditional recipes such as Tuscan *pan di ramerino* (rosemary buns) have been handed down and can still be found today.

There is an unmistakeable aroma of yeasty freshly baked bread when you enter a *forno* (bakery). It is so very warming and comforting. Traditional Italian bakeries have an oven on site, probably out the back, with a door or window through to the shop. If you position yourself at the right angle, you might even be able to see the fornaio at work, wearing one of those tall white *toque da cuochi* (chef's hats), and using a long paddle to retrieve bread from a wood-fired oven. You can tell a good forno by the queues of people you see waiting to buy bread and other baked goods in the morning, when loaves are still warm and at their fragrant best. Bread is often sold by weight and cut from a larger loaf. Italians tend to buy their bread daily and then use bread that is a day or two old for other purposes (like crostini).

The best time to visit a bakery is mid-morning, in time for that mid-morning *spuntino* (snack), although be prepared to wait in line. If you go towards lunchtime, you will probably be disappointed as the shelves will be bare. There are regional differences in bakery products which reflect traditions and make it delightful though sometimes confusing for tourists as there are so many different types of baked savoury snacks. You will find *schiacciata* (a type of focaccia) in Florence; *pizza bianca* (plain pizza) in Rome; *taralli* (rings of crisp dough, boiled then baked) in Puglia and *fiadoni* (half moons of thin bread-like dough enveloping a cheesy eggy centre) in Abruzzo. If you're not sure what to buy, just look at what the person next to you is buying (especially if they are a local). They will undoubtedly know best.

FOCACCIA BARESE

{ FOCACCIA BARI-STYLE }

1 MEDIUM PONTIAC OR DESIREE POTATO

250 G (9 OZ/1²/₃ CUPS) 00 WEAK (CAKE) FLOUR OR PLAIN (ALL-PURPOSE) FLOUR, PLUS EXTRA FOR DUSTING

250 G (9 OZ/2 CUPS) FINE SEMOLINA

6 G (¼ OZ) INSTANT DRIED YEAST

1 TEASPOON SUGAR

350 ML (12 FL OZ) TEPID WATER

1 TEASPOON SALT

EXTRA-VIRGIN OLIVE OIL, FOR GREASING AND DRIZZLING

50 G (1¾ OZ) PITTED BLACK OLIVES, HALVED

200 G (7 OZ) RIPE CHERRY OR OTHER SMALL TOMATOES, HALVED OR QUARTERED

DRIED OREGANO, FOR SPRINKLING

I ate this focaccia for the first time in Bari from a little bakery called Panificio Santa Rita, in a tiny laneway, off the beaten track. It was mid-morning and I stood outside, as one elderly local after another emerged holding a slice of yeasty dough studded with bright red tomatoes. They stood in a circle outside, chatting between mouthfuls of focaccia. I found out from the fornaio (baker) that the dough is made with potatoes, and that I was lucky to have found any left, as he had usually sold out by this time. And I could see why – the centre of the focaccia was moist, the outside crisp, and the sweet tomatoes and salty olives made for a delicious snack. You can experiment with other toppings, but tomatoes, olives and oregano are traditional.

Place the potato in a small saucepan, fill with cold water and bring to the boil. Cook for about 30 minutes or until easily pierced with a fork. Drain, peel and mash or push through a potato ricer. You need 150 g (5½ oz) cooked potato.

Whisk the flour, semolina, dried yeast and sugar in a large bowl. Add the warm potato and tepid water. Stir through using a wooden spoon, then add the salt. Bring the dough together, then tip onto a well-floured work surface and knead for a few minutes until smooth. Divide the dough in half and fold the dough a couple of times.

Oil the base and sides of two 22 cm (8¾ in) cake tins. Place each mound of dough, seam side down, in the centre of each tin and cover with clean tea towels. Place in a draught-free spot for at least 1 hour or until doubled in size.

Preheat the oven to 200°C (400°F).

With well-oiled hands, lift the dough from the tins and flip onto the other side. Push the dough back into the tins using your fingers, so that they are covered in small indentations. Push olive and tomato halves in the indentations, then sprinkle over some dried oregano. Drizzle with extra-virgin olive oil.

Bake for 30 minutes, or until the focacce have risen and are golden on top. Enjoy warm.

MAKES 2 LARGE FOCACCE

CALZONE con CIPOLLA e OLIVE

{ ONION AND OLIVE CALZONE }

PASTRY

500 G (1 LB 2 OZ) PLAIN (ALL-PURPOSE) FLOUR, PLUS EXTRA FOR DUSTING

6 G (¼ OZ) INSTANT DRIED YEAST

90 ML (3 FL OZ) EXTRA-VIRGIN OLIVE OIL

200 ML (7 FL OZ) TEPID WATER

½ TEASPOON SALT

1 SMALL EGG, BEATEN WITH A SPLASH OF MILK

FILLING

2 TABLESPOONS OLIVE OIL, PLUS EXTRA FOR GREASING

400 G (14 OZ) LEEKS, WHITE PART ONLY, CLEANED AND SLICED

5 SPRING ONIONS, SLICED

600 G (1 LB 5 OZ) BROWN OR WHITE ONIONS, CHOPPED

100 G (3½ OZ) TINNED CHOPPED TOMATOES, DRAINED

50 G (1¾ OZ) SULTANAS (GOLDEN RAISINS)

100 G (3½ OZ) GREEN OLIVES, PITTED

½ TEASPOON SALT

½ TEASPOON PEPPER

10 ANCHOVIES

When we talk about 'calzone', we think of a pizza filled with cheese and other toppings, folded in half and baked. In the southern region of Puglia, calzone is something completely different. Panificio Fiore in the old town of Bari is well known for its calzone, with lunchtime queues snaking through the narrow streets. The onion calzone they sell by the slice is terrific, making a substantial on-the-go meal. This recipe uses sweet onions and sultanas (golden raisins), making a lovely contrast to the savoury olives and anchovies. It is delicious served with a green salad on the side.

To make the pastry, place the flour in a large bowl, sprinkle in the yeast and lightly whisk. Pour in the oil and mix using a wooden spoon and eventually your fingertips, until incorporated. Pour in the water, a little at a time, mixing it in with your hands, until well combined. Lastly, sprinkle over the salt, then tip onto a well-floured work surface and knead the dough for about 10 minutes until smooth and elastic. Alternatively, you can use a stand mixer with a dough hook attachment to make the dough. Don't worry if the mixture seems a bit on the dry side. Transfer the dough to a large bowl, cover with plastic wrap and set aside in a draught-free place for about 2 hours or until doubled in size.

Meanwhile, to make the filling, heat the oil in a heavy-based saucepan over low–medium heat. Add the leek, spring onion and onion and cook, covered, for about 30 minutes, stirring regularly. The onion should be soft, translucent and just starting to caramelise. Add the tomatoes, sultanas, olives, salt and pepper and cook for a further 15 minutes. If there is any excess liquid at the end of cooking, drain the mixture in a colander, then set aside to cool completely.

Preheat the oven to 180°C (350°F). Line the base and side of a 28 cm (11 in) tart tin with a removable base (I use foil). Lightly grease the tin with olive oil.

Divide the dough into two – one half should be slightly larger than the other. Roll out the larger piece of dough on a well-floured work surface to a 38 cm (15 in) circle. Transfer the dough to the tin, pushing gently into the base and side and allowing a bit of dough to hang over the edge. Place the cooled filling in the tart and arrange the anchovies on top in a radial pattern. Roll out the second piece of dough to a circle large enough to cover the filling. Place the dough over the filling and fold the excess pastry from the base onto the top of the calzone so that it is well sealed. Trim any excess pastry.

»

CALZONE con CIPOLLA e OLIVE

Make a central hole in the pastry lid using a sharp knife so that air can escape during cooking. Brush the egg and milk wash over the top.

Bake for about 1 hour or until the top is a deep golden colour and the pastry is cooked all the way through. The calzone will puff up quite a bit during cooking and fall again once it cools.

Eat warm or at room temperature. The calzone will keep, covered, for 3–4 days in the fridge.

SERVES 8

FIADONI ABRUZZESI

{ PUFFED CHEESE BITES }

DOUGH

300 G (10½ OZ/2 CUPS) PLAIN (ALL-PURPOSE)
FLOUR, PLUS EXTRA FOR DUSTING

3 EGGS, LIGHTLY BEATEN

100 ML (3½ FL OZ) OLIVE OIL

100 ML (3½ FL OZ) DRY WHITE WINE

SPLASH OF MILK

FILLING

175 G (6 OZ) RIGATINO CHEESE (OR SUBSTITUTE
PECORINO SARDO OR PECORINO TOSCANO),
GRATED

150 G (5½ OZ) PARMESAN, GRATED

2 EGGS, LIGHTLY BEATEN

4 G (¼ OZ) INSTANT DRIED YEAST

When I was in Abruzzo, I bought fiadoni from the forno that were warm, cheesy and so very light. Thin bread-like pastry is cut into circles and traditionally mounds of cheese and egg are placed in the centre, before closing the circle into a half moon, and making a pattern on the edges with a fork. Small incisions are made on the top of the fiadone to allow a little cheese to escape as they cook. These savoury fiadoni should not to be confused with sweet fiadoni from Corsica.

Place the flour and a pinch of salt in a large wide bowl. In a smaller bowl, whisk 2 of the eggs with the oil and wine. Make a well in the centre of the flour and pour in the egg mixture. Using a wooden spoon, bring the mixture together, then start using your hands to knead the dough. Tip onto a lightly floured work surface and knead for 2 minutes until smooth. The mix will be quite soft, stretchy and pliable. Cover in plastic wrap and set aside for 30 minutes while you make the filling.

To make the filling, combine the cheeses, egg, yeast and black pepper, to taste, in a bowl. Mix with a spoon to form a cohesive mass, then set aside.

Preheat the oven to 200°C (400°F). Line a baking tray with baking paper.

Divide the dough into two. Working with one piece at a time, roll out the dough on a lightly floured work surface to 2 mm (⅛ in) thick. The dough will be stretchy and sturdy. Cut out circles using a 10 cm (4 in) cookie cutter, then roll the individual circles a little more as they tend to bounce back. Place 1 tablespoon of filling in the centre of each circle, then fold over and pinch the dough with your fingers to seal, making sure you have not incorporated any air. Use the tines of a fork to press down and secure the edges further. Transfer to the prepared baking tray.

Whisk the remaining egg with the milk and lightly brush the tops of the fiadoni. Make a small incision in the top of each parcel.

Bake for 20–25 minutes or until pale golden on top and cooked through. The fiadoni will have puffed and crisped up, and may have split open a little (giving them a rustic look). They are best eaten when warm, but will keep in an airtight container for 1–2 days in the fridge.

MAKES 20–24

TARALLI NAPOLETANI

{ NEAPOLITAN TARALLI }

110 G (4 OZ) WHOLE ALMONDS (THE SMALLER THE BETTER)

500 G (1 LB 2 OZ) PLAIN (ALL-PURPOSE) FLOUR. PLUS EXTRA FOR DUSTING

8 G (⅓ OZ) INSTANT DRIED YEAST

210 ML (7 FL OZ) TEPID WATER

160 ML (5½ FL OZ) EXTRA-VIRGIN OLIVE OIL

2 TEASPOONS FRESHLY GROUND BLACK PEPPER

3 TEASPOONS SALT

SPLASH OF MILK. FOR BRUSHING

Taralli Napoletani are spicy savoury rings, traditionally made with strutto which is made from pork back fat. This makes them unbelievably crisp and delicious. Strutto however is not to everyone's liking (as well as being difficult to find outside of Italy), so the version below is made with olive oil. They are not as crisp as the ones you find on the streets of Naples but they are just as tasty and particularly suited to a glass of rosé and an evening with friends.

If your almonds are on the large side, cut them in half lengthways and set aside.

Whisk the flour and yeast together in a large bowl. Add the water and oil and mix with a wooden spoon. Add the pepper, salt and almonds and mix with your hands. Tip out onto a lightly floured work surface and knead for a couple of minutes until the mixture is homogenous and fairly smooth. Roll small balls of dough about 40 g (1½ oz) each and place on a baking tray lined with baking paper. Cover with a clean tea towel and set aside to rest for about 30 minutes.

Preheat the oven to 175°C (345°F).

Take a ball of dough and place it on a well-floured work surface. Using your fingertips, stretch out and roll the ball into a rope by moving your fingers outwards as they roll backwards and forwards. The rope should be 22–24 cm (8¾–9½ in) in length. Now twist along its length and join both ends to make a large ring. This can be a bit tricky as the almonds have a tendency to fall off. If they do, embed them back into the dough. Place on a baking tray lined with baking paper and repeat with the remaining balls of dough. Set the dough rings aside to rest, covered with a clean tea towel, for a further 30 minutes.

Brush the taralli with a little milk and bake for 40 minutes or until golden. Store in an airtight container for up to 1 week.

MAKES ABOUT 24

CRESCENTINE

{ PAN-COOKED FLAT BREAD }

250 G (9 OZ/1²/₃ CUPS) PLAIN (ALL-PURPOSE) FLOUR, PLUS EXTRA FOR DUSTING

3 G (¹/₈ OZ) INSTANT DRIED YEAST

85 ML (2¾ FL OZ) TEPID WATER

50 ML (1¾ FL OZ) TEPID MILK

3 TEASPOONS OLIVE OIL

1 TEASPOON SALT

12 THIN SLICES PROSCIUTTO OR LARDO, TO SERVE

200 G (7 OZ) BUFFALO MOZZARELLA (SEE PAGE 18) OR STRACCHINO, SLICED, OR 50 G (1¾ OZ) SHAVED PARMESAN

When travelling in Italy last year, I asked my friend Laura who lives in Bologna what she thought was the most popular street food where she lived. "Tigelle, without a doubt," she replied. "We eat them with a little prosciutto or cheese, and a glass of wine."

When I looked into tigelle I found out that this was actually the name of the traditional terracotta press they were made in; the bread is called crescentina or crescenza. That said, most people know them as tigelle. They are easy to make at home without a modern tigella iron as the yeasted dough can be cooked in a non-stick pan.

Place the flour and yeast in a medium-sized bowl and whisk lightly. In a separate bowl, mix together the water and milk, then stir into the flour. Add the oil and use your hands to bring the dough together. Tip the dough onto a lightly floured work surface and sprinkle over the salt. Knead for about 10 minutes until smooth and stretchy. Alternatively, you can make the dough in a stand mixer with a dough hook attachment. Transfer to a large bowl, cover with plastic wrap and set aside in a warm draught-free spot for at least 1 hour or until doubled in size.

On a lightly floured work surface, roll out the dough until it is 3–4 mm (¼ in) thick. Cut out circles of dough using an 8 cm (3¼ in) cookie cutter. Re-roll the off-cuts to make as many circles as possible.

Heat a large non-stick frying pan over low–medium heat. Cook the dough, in batches, for about 3 minutes on each side until cooked through. They should puff up nicely and turn golden in colour.

Cut in half through the centre (like you would a bread roll) and eat warm filled with prosciutto or other cured meat and a soft cheese such as fresh buffalo mozzarella or stracchino. My favourite filling is thinly sliced lardo and shaved parmesan cheese.

MAKES 10–12

RUSTICO LECCESE

{ RUSTICO PASTRY }

20 G (¾ OZ) UNSALTED BUTTER

20 G (¾ OZ) PLAIN (ALL-PURPOSE) FLOUR, PLUS EXTRA FOR DUSTING

120 ML (4 FL OZ) MILK

PINCH OF GROUND NUTMEG

80 G (2¾ OZ) AGED MOZZARELLA CHEESE OR SCAMORZA (SEE PAGES 18–19), AT ROOM TEMPERATURE, CUT INTO SMALL CUBES

200 G (7 OZ) TINNED CHOPPED TOMATOES

½ TEASPOON EXTRA-VIRGIN OLIVE OIL

375 G (13 OZ) STORE-BOUGHT PUFF PASTRY

1 SMALL EGG, LIGHTLY BEATEN

Rustico Leccese is a typical street food from Lecce in Puglia. It is a bit like a vol-au-vent with a lid, but a very Italian one, filled with mozzarella cheese, tomato and béchamel sauce. You can use store-bought butter puff pastry to make your rustici.

To prepare the béchamel sauce, melt the butter with the flour in a small saucepan over low heat, stirring the whole time until the mixture looks like wet sand. Slowly pour in the milk, a little at a time, stirring continuously, until incorporated. Keep stirring for a few minutes until the mixture thickens. Remove from the heat and stir through a good pinch of salt and the nutmeg. Add the mozzarella and stir until melted. Transfer to a small bowl and set aside to cool.

Place the chopped tomatoes in a colander and press down hard to remove as much excess liquid as possible. Transfer to a bowl, add the olive oil and salt and pepper, to taste, and mix well. Set aside.

Roll out the puff pastry on a lightly floured work surface until it is 3 mm (⅛ in) thick. Using an 8 cm (3¼ in) and a 10 cm (4 in) cookie cutter, cut out 6 circles of each size. The smaller circle will form the base of the rustico and the larger circle will form the lid. You might need to re-roll the pastry scraps to make the correct number of circles. Place the smaller circles on a baking tray lined with baking paper.

Place 2 teaspoons of the cooled béchamel on each of the smaller circles, leaving a 1 cm (½ in) border. Place 2 teaspoons of the tomato mixture on top of the béchamel, then dip a small brush (or your finger) in the egg and run it around the edge of each circle. Place the larger pastry circles on top and press the circles together with your fingers. Brush the top of each rustico with egg, then set aside in the fridge for at least 45 minutes to 1 hour to firm up the pastry.

Preheat the oven to 200°C (400°F).

Bake the rustici for 20 minutes or until they are puffed up and golden. Set aside to cool for 5–10 minutes before eating.

MAKES 8

TARALLINI PUGLIESI

{ LITTLE TARALLI FROM PUGLIA }

500 G (1 LB 2 OZ) PLAIN (ALL-PURPOSE) FLOUR, PLUS EXTRA FOR DUSTING

200 ML (7 FL OZ) DRY WHITE WINE, AT ROOM TEMPERATURE

130 ML (4½ FL OZ) EXTRA-VIRGIN OLIVE OIL

1 TEASPOON SEA SALT

1½ TEASPOONS FENNEL SEEDS

Tarallini are small taralli typical of Puglia, on the Southern Adriatic coast of Italy. They are usually flavoured with fennel seeds, but you can use also use chilli flakes or pepper. Boiling and baking the tarallini makes them quite crisp and an ideal accompaniment to a glass of wine.

Place all of the ingredients in a large bowl and stir with a wooden spoon until well incorporated. Tip the dough onto a lightly floured work surface and knead for about 12 minutes. Alternatively, you can use a stand mixer with a dough hook attachment. The dough will be smooth and soft.

Break off balls of dough about 25 g (1 oz) in weight, then roll each ball into a 10 cm (4 in) baton. Join the two ends by overlapping them slightly and pressing together to make a circle. Repeat until you have about 35 rings.

Bring a medium-sized saucepan of water to the boil. Cook the dough rings in batches of 5–7 for about 1 minute or until they float to the surface. Remove with a slotted spoon and place on a clean tea towel to drain any excess water, then transfer to a wire rack and place in a cold oven with the door slightly open for 8 hours or overnight.

Remove the dough rings from the oven and preheat the oven to 200°C (400°F). Line a baking tray with baking paper.

Place the tarallini on the prepared tray and bake for 30–35 minutes until golden and cooked through – test one by breaking it in half to check it is cooked). Cool on a wire rack.

The tarallini will keep for several weeks in an airtight container.

MAKES ABOUT 35

ROSETTE di PANE

{ ROSETTA BREAD ROLLS }

500 G (1 LB 2 OZ) STRONG BREAD FLOUR
(SEE PAGE 17)

5 G (¼ OZ) FRESH YEAST, CRUMBLED

50 G (1¾ OZ) PLAIN (ALL-PURPOSE) FLOUR

25 ML (¾ FL OZ) WATER

1 TEASPOON SUGAR

2 TEASPOONS SALT

OLIVE OIL, FOR BRUSHING

Rosette are rose-shaped bread rolls also known as rosette soffiate, which means blown or puffed up. They have quite a hard crust and should be hollow inside, making them perfect for filling with all sorts of goodies such as porchetta (page 143) or tartufata (page 104). They take a couple of days to make, and it is the only recipe in this book where I use fresh yeast. Such a special dish deserves the real thing and I have not been able to recreate them with instant dried yeast. I also recommend you use a stand mixer with a dough hook for this recipe. I made the shape of the bread using an apple cutter (available from most cooking shops).

If your rolls are not hollow inside, don't worry too much, just remove some of the mollica (soft bread in the centre) to make space for your filling.

Place the strong flour, 250 ml (8½ fl oz/1 cup) water and fresh yeast into the bowl of a stand mixer and mix with a dough hook on low speed for 5 minutes. The resulting dough will be quite soft but not particularly smooth. Transfer to a bowl, cover with plastic wrap and set aside to rest in a warm spot for 16–18 hours.

Return the dough to your stand mixer, add the remaining ingredients except the olive oil and mix with a dough hook on low speed for 14 minutes. The dough should be smooth and quite soft. Transfer to a clean work surface and roll 80 g (2¾ oz) balls of dough with the palms of your hands, making sure each ball is smooth.

Brush the balls with olive oil, then flatten with the palm of your hand. Using an apple cutter or similar, stamp the surface of each rosetta by cutting down to almost the base of the bread but not all the way through. Turn the ball of dough over so that the 'rose' shape is on the bottom and place, well spaced, on baking trays lined with baking paper. Cover with a damp clean tea towel and set aside in a warm place to prove for 2–3 hours.

Preheat the oven to 220°C (430°F). Place a small heatproof glass of water on a separate baking tray and place at the back of the oven. (The water serves to steam the outside of the bread so the crust becomes hard).

Bake the rosette for 22 minutes, until golden. Transfer to a wire rack to cool.

MAKES 10

PAN di RAMERINO

{ROSEMARY BUNS}

200 G (7 OZ) SULTANAS (GOLDEN RAISINS)

125 ML (4 FL OZ/½ CUP) VIN SANTO (DESSERT WINE)

250 G (9 OZ/1⅔ CUPS) 00 WEAK (CAKE) FLOUR (SEE PAGE 17), PLUS EXTRA FOR DUSTING

250 G (9 OZ/1⅔ CUPS) STRONG BREAD FLOUR (SEE PAGE 17)

5 G (¼ OZ) INSTANT DRIED YEAST

100 G (3½ OZ) CASTER (SUPERFINE) SUGAR

170 ML (5½ FL OZ/⅔ CUP) TEPID WATER

2 SCANT TEASPOONS SALT

1 EGG YOLK, BEATEN WITH 1 TABLESPOON WATER

ROSEMARY OIL

100 ML (3½ FL OZ) GOOD-QUALITY EXTRA-VIRGIN OLIVE OIL

20 G (¾ OZ) ROSEMARY LEAVES

SUGAR SYRUP

110 G (4 OZ/½ CUP) SUGAR

½ TEASPOON VANILLA BEAN PASTE

An Australian friend living in Florence introduced me to this bread. We had spent the day together looking at delicatessens and bakeries and she handed me a bag containing pan di ramerino, 'in case you get hungry on the journey back to Rome'. I thanked her but thought how unlikely that would be, as we had spent the whole day eating. As soon as I opened the paper bag and smelled the sweet rosemary, I couldn't resist eating it immediately.

To make the rosemary oil, place the oil and rosemary leaves in a small saucepan over low heat. Infuse at this temperature for 10 minutes. Remove from the heat and strain the oil using a fine-meshed sieve. Set the oil aside and discard the rosemary.

Place the sultanas in a bowl with 125 ml (4 fl oz/½ cup) water and the vin santo. Set aside for 15 minutes, then drain and squeeze the sultanas to remove any excess liquid.

Place the flours, yeast and sugar in a large bowl and whisk to combine. Add the tepid water and stir using a wooden spoon. Add the rosemary oil and salt and incorporate well. Tip the dough onto a floured work surface and knead for 5 minutes or until smooth. Add the sultanas and knead for a further 5 minutes. Transfer to a bowl, cover with plastic wrap and set aside in a warm place for 2 hours, by which time it should have increased in size (but not quite doubled).

Divide the dough into twelve balls and transfer to a baking tray lined with baking paper. Cover with a tea towel and set aside to rest in a draught-free spot for 1 hour.

Brush the egg wash on the buns, then cover in plastic wrap and set aside to rest for a further 30 minutes. Preheat the oven to 200°C (400°F).

To make traditional-looking pan di ramerino, make a criss-cross pattern on the bread using the sharp point of a knife. Bake for 20–25 minutes, or until golden brown.

Meanwhile, make the sugar syrup. Combine the sugar, vanilla bean paste and 125 ml (4 fl oz/½ cup) water in a small saucepan and bring to the boil. Reduce the heat and simmer for about 8 minutes, until reduced by half.

Transfer the buns to a wire rack and brush over the sugar syrup. Eat while warm for morning tea or as part of a European-style breakfast.

MAKES 12

IL PASTICCIE

{ SWEET TREATS }

Rococò
Sweet Christmas taralli

Babà al rhum
Rum baba

Cassatelle
Sweet fried pastries with lemon ricotta

Crema fritta
Fried custard

Fritole Triestine
Apple fritters

Sfogliatelle con pasta frolla
Shortcrust pastry sfogliatelle

Ciambelle
Ring doughnuts

Raviole Bolognesi
Sweet pastry raviole

Cannoli al cacao con ricotta
Cocoa cannoli with ricotta

Crostoli
Sweet fried pastry wings

Torcinelli
Potato fritters with aniseed

Taralli al limone
Lemon taralli

Pardule
Sardinian ricotta cakes

Castagnole di ricotta
Sweet ricotta balls

The cakes and sweets found at traditional Italian street fairs were made for the celebration of Carnevale, which is held in the days leading up to Lent. The frittolaro from the Veneto region and the zeppolaio from around Naples would be given the best spot in the piazza or along the road, to cook and sell their sweet fragrant balls of yeasty dough called frittelle (or fritole) and zeppole, freshly fried in a vat of hot oil. Both are a fritter or doughnut of sorts, made with flour, eggs and sugar, often laced with dried fruit and citrus zest.

Many Italian fried sweets are typical of the Lenten season and one of the best-loved is the Sicilian cannolo. With origins dating to the Arab conquest of Sicily, some say that the women in a harem in Caltanisetta combined Roman and Arab dishes to create tubes of pastry filled with creamy sweet ricotta; while others claim the cannolo was born in the convents, after the dissolution of harems. Despite its uncertain origins, the cannolo has survived to become one of Italy's best-loved sweet street foods. There are even fairs dedicated to the cannolo such as the Sagra del Cannolo Siciliano in Palermo, where cannoli are made by filling fried sweet pastry tubes with sweet fresh sheep's milk ricotta and decorated with nuts.

Most traditional fried and baked sweets can now be found throughout the year in *pasticcerie* (pastry/cake shops), where the *pasticciere* (pastry cook) has taken over from the frittolaro, the zeppolaio and the women in harems and convents.

Italians love eating sweet pastries for breakfast, so the day of a pasticciere starts very early in the morning as jam-filled *cornetti* (Italian croissants) and vanilla custard-filled *bomboloni* (doughnuts) are delivered to local bars before they start filling up with caffeine-deprived, hungry Italians just starting their day.

ROCOCÒ

{ SWEET CHRISTMAS TARALLI }

350 G (12½ OZ) BLANCHED ALMONDS

500 G (1 LB 2 OZ) 00 WEAK (CAKE) FLOUR

200 G (7 OZ) SUGAR

2 SCANT TEASPOONS BAKING POWDER

ZEST OF 2 ORANGES

ZEST OF 1 LEMON

20 G (¾ OZ) PISTO (SEE BELOW)

PINCH OF SALT

100 G (3½ OZ) HONEY

2 EGGS – 1 LIGHTLY BEATEN; 1 BEATEN WITH
A SPLASH OF MILK

PISTO

4 G (¼ OZ) STAR ANISE

4 G (¼ OZ) FRESHLY GRATED NUTMEG

4 G (¼ OZ) GROUND CINNAMON

4 G (¼ OZ) CLOVES

4 G (¼ OZ) WHITE PEPPER

Rococò are dense, hard, spicy ring-shaped biscotti that are eaten on the streets of Naples around Christmas time. They contain a typical Neapolitan spice mix called 'pisto', which is used in certain traditional pastries. Pisto is hard to find ready prepared outside of Naples, but you can easily make your own using equal quantities of star anise, nutmeg, cinnamon, cloves and white pepper.

Preheat the oven to 200°C (400°F).

To make the pisto, combine all of the ingredients in a mortar and pestle and grind to a fine powder.

Place the almonds on a baking tray and roast for 15–20 minutes, checking on them every few minutes and tossing them around, until they look golden and a lovely almond smell fills the room. Transfer to a heatproof bowl and set aside to cool.

Once cool, reserve about 25 almonds, then place the rest in a food processor and finely process. Roughly chop the reserved almonds to use as decoration.

Place the flour, sugar, processed almonds, baking powder, zests, pisto and salt in a large bowl. Give the ingredients a good whisk then turn out onto a clean work surface. Make a well in the centre and add the honey and the beaten egg. Work this through the dry ingredients with your fingers, then start adding 125 ml (4 fl oz/½ cup) water, a little at a time, until it is all incorporated. The dough should be quite stiff but homogenous.

Reduce the oven temperature to 180°C (350°F). Line a baking tray with baking paper.

Using your hands, take 50 g (1¾ oz) balls of dough and roll them into sausages. Join the two ends to make 8 cm (3¼ in) rings. Decorate each ring with the reserved almond pieces, then brush with the egg and milk wash and place on the prepared baking tray.

Bake for about 20 minutes, until deep golden. For a harder rococò, bake for a couple of minutes longer. The rococò will keep in an airtight container for up to 1 week.

MAKES ABOUT 24

BABÀ al RHUM

{ RUM BABA }

450 G (1 LB) STRONG (BAKER'S) FLOUR (SEE PAGE 17)

10 G (⅓ OZ) INSTANT DRIED YEAST

80 G (2¾ OZ/⅔ CUP) CASTER (SUPERFINE) SUGAR

6 EGGS

170 ML (5½ FL OZ/⅔ CUP) TEPID MILK

150 G (5½ OZ) BUTTER, AT ROOM TEMPERATURE, DICED, PLUS EXTRA FOR GREASING

1 TEASPOON SALT

500 G (1 LB 2 OZ) GRANULATED SUGAR

PEEL OF 1 ORANGE, WHITE PITH REMOVED, CUT INTO THIN STRIPS

250 ML (8½ FL OZ/1 CUP) DARK RUM

WHIPPED CREAM, TO SERVE (OPTIONAL)

The historic centre of Naples is a magical and musical hub of activity, where street food reigns until late at night, every night. Pasticcerie (pastry shops) with benches facing the street sell desserts until late, and rum babas are one of the most popular. Locals effortlessly balance and eat their babas with rum syrup and whipped cream as they stand chatting.

You will need baba moulds (which you can purchase from shops that sell Italian cooking equipment) or 100 ml (3½ fl oz) capacity dariole moulds to make this recipe. A similar capacity muffin or popover pan can work too, although the shape will not be as traditional. Rum babas are lots of fun and a bit retro. I love adding orange peel to the rum syrup, which isn't traditional but gives the syrup extra depth.

Place half the flour, the yeast, sugar, eggs and milk in the bowl of a stand mixer and mix on high speed for 4 minutes until the dough is stretchy and elastic. You can also use a hand-held mixer or a hand-held whisk with a good deal of energy. On a low speed, add the butter, one piece at a time, incorporating each piece fully before adding the next. Mix for a further 2 minutes on high speed, then add the remaining flour and the salt. Continue beating for a few more minutes until the dough thickens. Cover with plastic wrap and set aside to rest for 1 hour.

Meanwhile, butter the base and side of the baba or dariole moulds.

Once the dough has rested, mix for another 2 minutes on medium speed.

Preheat the oven to 190°C (375°F).

Divide the dough evenly among the moulds, filling them just under three-quarters full. Transfer the moulds to a baking tray and cover with a clean tea towel. Set aside to rest in a draught-free spot for a further 30 minutes.

Transfer the baking tray to the oven and bake for about 15 minutes until the babas are cooked through, golden and puffed up.

»

BABÀ al RHUM

Immediately, remove the babas from the moulds and set aside to cool.

To make a syrup, place the granulated sugar, orange peel and 500 ml (17 fl oz/2 cups) water in a saucepan over medium heat and cook, stirring occasionally, until the sugar dissolves. Add the rum and cook for a further 5 minutes. Remove from the heat and set aside.

Dip the cooled babas, one at a time, in the syrup until they are wet. Don't leave them in there for too long or they may start to crumble. Place on a wire rack with a plate underneath to drain off excess syrup.

If you have any remaining syrup, cook it over a medium heat for a few minutes until it reduces and thickens a little. Pour it on individual babas when serving.

Serve the babas warm or cold with whipped cream on the side, if using, and the reduced syrup poured over the top.

Rum babas will keep in an airtight container in the fridge for 1–2 days. To serve warm, gently reheat in a microwave oven.

MAKES ABOUT 16

CASSATELLE

{ SWEET FRIED PASTRIES WITH LEMON RICOTTA }

1 EGG WHITE, FOR BRUSHING

GRAPESEED, PEANUT OR SUNFLOWER OIL,
FOR DEEP-FRYING

ICING (CONFECTIONERS') SUGAR, FOR DUSTING

PASTRY

250 G (9 OZ/1²/₃ CUPS) 00 WEAK (CAKE) FLOUR
(SEE PAGE 17), PLUS EXTRA FOR DUSTING

30 G (1 OZ) CASTER (SUPERFINE) SUGAR

PINCH OF SALT

2 TEASPOONS EXTRA-VIRGIN OLIVE OIL

1 TABLESPOON MARSALA

FILLING

200 G (7 OZ) FRESH DRAINED RICOTTA
(SEE PAGE 18)

30 G (1 OZ) CASTER (SUPERFINE) SUGAR

ZEST OF 1 LEMON

¼ TEASPOON VANILLA ESSENCE

1 TEASPOON HONEY

Cassatelle are known as cassateddi in Sicilian dialect and are typical of the area around Trapani. They are sweet ravioli filled with a sweet ricotta cream. The ricotta needs to be quite dry, so make sure you buy the type that has been drained in a perforated basket. The less traditional filling of lemon and ricotta is quite delightful, although you can easily substitute the lemon zest, honey and vanilla with 30 g (1 oz) of chopped dark chocolate and an extra teaspoon of sugar, for a more traditional version.

To make the pastry, sift the flour into a medium-sized bowl and whisk in the sugar and salt. Using a wooden spoon, mix in the olive oil and Marsala and gradually add 130 ml (4½ fl oz) water until it forms a cohesive mass. Tip out onto a clean work surface and knead the dough for about 2 minutes until it is smooth and soft. Transfer to a bowl, cover with plastic wrap and set aside to rest for 30 minutes.

To make the filling, place all of the ingredients in a bowl and mash with a fork until smooth. Alternatively, combine the ingredients in a food processor. Set aside until ready to use.

Cut the dough in half, then roll out one half on a lightly floured work surface to 2 mm (¹/₁₆ in) thick. Cut out circles of dough using a 9 cm (3½ in) round cookie cutter. Place 2 heaped teaspoons of the ricotta filling on each circle and lightly run your finger dipped in egg white around the rim. Fold the circle of dough in half enclosing the ricotta and press down gently to seal, making sure no air is trapped inside. Place on a lightly floured baking tray and repeat for the remaining cassatelle. You can knead and roll out the scraps of dough to make additional cassatelle.

Place plenty of oil in a small saucepan with a high side or use a deep-fryer. Heat the oil to 170°C (340°F) or until a scrap of dough dropped into the oil bubbles immediately. Cook the cassatelle in batches of 2–3 for 3½–4 minutes, turning halfway, until golden brown all over. Drain on kitchen towel and set aside to cool slightly.

Dust with icing sugar and serve warm.

MAKES ABOUT 24

Taralli
Napoletani
€ 16.00 il Kg

CREMA FRITTA

{ FRIED CUSTARD }

500 ML (17 FL OZ/2 CUPS FULL-CREAM (WHOLE) MILK

PEEL OF 1 LEMON, WHITE PITH REMOVED

1 TEASPOON VANILLA BEAN PASTE

85 G (3 OZ) PLAIN (ALL-PURPOSE) FLOUR, SIFTED

40 G (1½ OZ) CORNFLOUR (CORNSTARCH), SIFTED

100 G (3½ OZ) CASTER (SUPERFINE) SUGAR

PINCH OF SALT

2 EGGS PLUS 2 EGG YOLKS

25 G (1 OZ) UNSALTED BUTTER

100 G (3½ OZ/1 CUP) FINE BREADCRUMBS

GRAPESEED, PEANUT OR SUNFLOWER OIL, FOR FRYING

When my mother was a little girl, she would eat crema fritta sold in the street markets in the Veneto region. Hard-set custard and fried until golden, they made a delicious sweet treat to enjoy in the cold Veneto winter. I love adding vanilla and lemon zest to the custard, making them even more moreish.

Line a rectangular baking dish (approximately 26 cm x 8 cm/10¼ in x 3¼ in) with a double layer of plastic wrap that hangs over the edges of the dish.

Place the milk, lemon peel and vanilla in a small saucepan over low heat. Heat the milk to just before boiling point, then remove from the heat and set aside, covered.

Place the sifted flours, sugar and salt in a large bowl, then whisk in the whole eggs and egg yolks, one at a time, until thoroughly combined.

Strain the milk into the batter in a slow steady stream, whisking the whole time – you do not want any lumps to form. Scrape the whole lot back into the saucepan then return to the stovetop over a low heat, stirring continuously and vigorously until the mixture comes to the boil and starts to thicken and becomes difficult to stir. This should take about 10 minutes. Allow to boil and bubble for a minute, stirring vigorously the whole time, even though it will be very stiff – this step is critical in making sure that the custard sets.

Remove from the heat and stir in the butter. Place into your prepared dish and flatten with a spatula. The custard should be 1.5 cm–2 cm (½ in–¾ in) thick. Cover the surface of the custard with plastic wrap and set aside to cool and solidify for about 4 hours (transfer to the fridge once the custard has cooled sufficiently).

Place the breadcrumbs on a plate. Remove the set custard from the dish using the overhanging plastic wrap. Cut into 5 cm (2 in) diamond shapes or squares, then toss thoroughly in the breadcrumbs.

Heat 4–5 cm (1½–2 in) oil in a heavy-based saucepan (or use a deep-fryer) to 180°C (350°F), or until a cube of bread dropped into the oil sizzles immediately. Cook the custard shapes in batches for about 2 minutes until light golden. Drain on kitchen towel and serve hot.

MAKES ABOUT 20

FRITOLE TRIESTINE

{APPLE FRITTERS}

1 EGG

60 ML (2 FL OZ/¼ CUP) FULL-CREAM (WHOLE) MILK

125 G (4½ OZ) PLAIN (ALL-PURPOSE) FLOUR, PLUS 1–2 TABLESPOONS EXTRA, IF NEEDED

1 SCANT TEASPOON BAKING POWDER

50 G (1¾ OZ) CASTER (SUPERFINE) SUGAR

PINCH OF SALT

2 TABLESPOONS SULTANAS (GOLDEN RAISINS), SOAKED IN 60 ML (2 FL OZ/¼ CUP) GRAPPA, BRANDY OR WARM WATER FOR 15 MINUTES

1 TART GREEN APPLE, SUCH AS GRANNY SMITH, PEELED AND CORED

ZEST OF ½ LARGE ORANGE

ZEST OF ½ LARGE LEMON

GRAPESEED, PEANUT OR SUNFLOWER OIL, FOR FRYING

ICING (CONFECTIONERS') SUGAR, FOR DUSTING

Fritole di mele are traditionally made around Carnevale (the period preceding Lent) but nowadays they are found throughout the year. I ate them at a marketplace by the port in the north-eastern Italian town of Trieste, and they were being bought as quickly as they were being fried. This is my mother's recipe and the method is not traditional, but they work well as long as you adjust the mixture with a bit of extra flour (if your egg is larger than most or if the apple is particularly juicy). The dough is fairly wet but should remain in an approximate ball when you drop tablespoons of the mixture in hot oil. I use grappa-soaked sultanas in this recipe (I always have a jar in the fridge), but if you do not have grappa or do not like the taste, use brandy or even warm water.

Place the egg and milk in a small bowl and whisk with a fork. Place the flour, baking powder, sugar and salt in a medium-sized bowl and whisk to combine. Mix the egg and milk into the flour and stir until it is homogenous.

Drain and squeeze the sultanas and grate the apple. Add these to the dough along with the zests and stir well to combine – the mixture should be thick but pourable. Add a bit of extra flour if it is too liquid.

Heat 4–5 cm (1½–2 in) oil in a heavy-based saucepan (or use a deep-fryer) to 170°C (340°F) or until a cube of bread dropped into the oil sizzles in 5 seconds. Using two metal tablespoons dipped in the hot oil, pick up a ball of mixture with one spoon, and push it into the hot oil with the other spoon. The balls should be as big as an apricot. Don't worry if you get little trails of dough. Cook 3–4 at a time, depending on the size of your pan, for about 4 minutes, until golden brown all over. Drain on kitchen towel and break open a fritola to check that it is cooked through. If it isn't, reduce the temperature of your oil slightly and wait a minute or two.

Once the fritole have cooled slightly, dust with icing sugar and serve warm.

Fritole are best eaten on the day they are made.

MAKES ABOUT 15

SFOGLIATELLE con PASTA FROLLA

{ SHORTCRUST PASTRY SFOGLIATELLE }

1 EGG YOLK, BEATEN WITH A SPLASH OF MILK

ICING (CONFECTIONERS') SUGAR, FOR DUSTING

PASTRY

500 G (1 LB 2 OZ) 00 WEAK (CAKE) FLOUR
(SEE PAGE 17),
PLUS EXTRA FOR DUSTING

170 G (6 OZ/¾ CUP) CASTER (SUPERFINE)
SUGAR

PINCH OF SALT

½ TEASPOON PURE VANILLA ESSENCE

200 G (7 OZ) COLD UNSALTED BUTTER, DICED

100 ML (3½ FL OZ) COLD WATER

FILLING

300 ML (10 FL OZ) FULL-CREAM (WHOLE)
MILK (OPTIONAL), PLUS EXTRA FOR SEALING
THE DOUGH

SALT

300 G (10½ OZ) FINE SEMOLINA

250 G (9 OZ) RICOTTA (SEE PAGE 18)

180 G (6½ OZ) CASTER (SUPERFINE) SUGAR

2 EGG YOLKS

¼ TEASPOON ORANGE BLOSSOM WATER

1½ TABLESPOONS CANDIED ORANGE PEEL,
FINELY CHOPPED

PINCH OF GROUND CINNAMON

Two varieties of sfogliatelle are eaten in Naples – the riccia and the frolla. Riccia have fan-shaped layers of filo-like pastry and, when eaten warm, are quite crisp. Frolla are made with thin shortcrust pastry. Both have the same sweet semolina and ricotta filling with candied citrus zest. Apparently, you are either a riccia fan or a frolla fan, and the fan-shaped riccia seem to be the most popular. I swim against the tide and admit to being a frolla fan. Traditionally, strutto (pork back fat) was used to make the pastry, but I have substituted this with butter. The sfogliatelle will keep for about 3 days in a sealed container, and are even nicer if you warm them up slightly. If you have a sweet tooth, re-dust with icing sugar before eating.

You will need to start this recipe a day ahead.

To make the pastry, place the flour, sugar and salt in a large bowl. Whisk briefly, then tip the lot onto a clean work surface and make a well in the centre. Scatter the vanilla essence and cold diced butter into the well and work into the flour quickly using your fingertips. Once the butter is incorporated and the mixture has a sandy texture, pour over the cold water, a little at a time, while you continue to work the dough. You should eventually have a cohesive smooth ball of dough. Scrape up any excess dough and pat onto the ball. Wrap in plastic wrap and set aside in the fridge overnight.

Combine the milk (if using) with 300 ml (10 fl oz) water in a large saucepan over medium heat. Alternatively, bring 600 ml (20½ fl oz) water to the boil. Add a pinch of salt, then slowly and steadily pour in the semolina, whisking constantly until it thickens. When it becomes too thick to use a whisk, change to a wooden spoon. This step is critical to ensure that your semolina is smooth and free of lumps. Once the semolina is completely incorporated, cook for about 5 minutes, stirring the mass until thick and stiff. Scrape into a heatproof bowl and set aside to cool to room temperature.

In a separate bowl, combine the ricotta, sugar, egg yolks, orange blossom water, candied peel, cinnamon and a pinch of salt, then add the semolina. As the semolina will be fairly stiff you will need to mix it in with your hands until it is homogeneous. Cover the bowl with plastic wrap and set aside in the fridge overnight.

>>

SFOGLIATELLE con PASTA FROLLA

Preheat the oven to 180°C (350°F). Line a baking tray with baking paper.

Bring the filling to room temperature. Divide the pastry in half, keeping the half you are not working on well wrapped in plastic wrap. On a well-floured work surface, divide one pastry half into 10 equal-sized pieces, then roll each piece out to a rectangle about 18 cm x 12 cm (7 in x 4¾ in).

Place an apricot-sized ball of the semolina mixture just off-centre on a rectangle of dough. Flatten the mixture slightly, then fold over the long edges of the pastry to obtain a pocket, about 7–8 cm (2¾–3¼ in) in diameter. Seal the edges with a little milk or water, then using a 9 cm (3½ in) cookie cutter or a glass of similar size cut out circles of sfogliatelle. Transfer to the prepared baking tray, then repeat with the remaining pastry and filling. Brush the surface of the sfogliatelle with the beaten egg yolk and milk and bake in two batches for 20–23 minutes until golden.

Set aside to cool on a wire rack for 30 minutes then dust with icing sugar. Ideally these should be served just warm and re-dusted with icing sugar.

The sfogliatelle will keep in an airtight container for 2–3 days.

MAKES 18–20

CIAMBELLE

{ RING DOUGHNUTS }

325 G (11½ OZ) PLAIN (ALL-PURPOSE) FLOUR,
PLUS EXTRA FOR DUSTING

2 G (⅛ G) INSTANT DRIED YEAST

50 G (1¾ OZ) CASTER (SUPERFINE) SUGAR,
PLUS EXTRA FOR DUSTING

ZEST OF ½ ORANGE

1 EGG, LIGHTLY BEATEN

140 ML (4½ FL OZ) TEPID MILK

¼ TEASPOON SALT

50 G (1¾ OZ) UNSALTED BUTTER, AT ROOM
TEMPERATURE, DICED

GRAPESEED, PEANUT OR SUNFLOWER OIL,
FOR FRYING

Ciambelle are similar to big ring doughnuts and are often eaten wrapped in a paper napkin standing up at the bar with a coffee. If you are lucky enough to turn up when they are freshly cooked and still warm, they are very moreish – so light and sweet, you would never guess they are deep-fried.

Combine the flour, yeast, sugar and orange zest in a large bowl. Add the egg and stir with a wooden spoon, then slowly pour in the milk, stirring the whole time. Finally, stir in the salt. Place the dough on a well-floured work surface and knead for a few minutes until smooth. Add a cube of butter and work it through the dough until incorporated. Work in the rest of the butter, one cube at a time, and knead until the dough is smooth and shiny. Alternatively, make the dough in a stand mixer with a dough hook attachment.

Place the dough in a large bowl and cover with plastic wrap. Set aside to rest in a draught-free place for 3 hours. It should more than double in size.

Divide the dough in half, keeping the half you are not working on well wrapped in plastic wrap. On a well floured work surface, roll the dough out to a thickness of 5–6 mm (¼ in). The dough is quite stretchy, so allow it to spring back before cutting. Using two cookie cutters (one at least twice as large as the other), cut circles and then small circles in the centres to make doughnut rings. If you prefer, you can incorporate the dough 'holes' back into the main dough and roll out again, or else you can keep them to cook. Repeat with the remaining dough. Place the ciambelle onto baking trays lined with baking paper and cover with clean tea towels. Place in a draught-free spot to rise for a couple of hours or until doubled in size.

Heat about 7 cm (2¾ in) of oil in a medium-sized saucepan or deep-fryer to 170°C (340°F) or until a cube of bread dropped into the oil sizzles in 5 seconds. Deep-fry the ciambelle 1–2 at a time for 3–4 minutes, flipping them over halfway until pale golden.

Drain the doughnuts on kitchen towel and set aside to cool a little. Serve warm, dusted with caster sugar, or dip them in caster sugar just before eating. Ciambelle are best eaten on the day they are made.

MAKES 16–18

RAVIOLE BOLOGNESI

{ SWEET PASTRY RAVIOLE }

250 G (9 OZ/1⅔ CUPS) 00 WEAK (CAKE) FLOUR (SEE PAGE 17), PLUS EXTRA FOR DUSTING

90 G (3 OZ) CASTER (SUPERFINE) SUGAR, PLUS EXTRA FOR SPRINKLING

1 TEASPOON BAKING POWDER

ZEST OF ½ LEMON

PINCH OF SALT

100 G (3½ OZ) BUTTER, AT ROOM TEMPERATURE, CUT INTO SMALL DICE

1 EGG, LIGHTLY BEATEN

190 G (6½ OZ) PLUM MOSTARDA OR YOUR FAVOURITE PLUM JAM

MILK, FOR BRUSHING

BITTER ALMOND LIQUEUR (OPTIONAL)

ANISEED LIQUEUR (OPTIONAL)

Raviole are bite-sized treats from Bologna in central Italy. They are traditionally eaten at the feast of San Giuseppe in March, although they can be found in shops and bars in the old market of Bologna all year round and make a great sweet snack. Raviole are not to be confused with savoury ravioli made from pasta, although the concept is similar. Raviole are made with a sweet shortcrust pastry, flavoured with lemon zest, and filled with a jam made of mustard fruits. They can also be made with plum jam, which is easier to find outside of Italy. During my research for this dish, I found a recipe that brushed aniseed and bitter almond liqueurs on the raviole once they were cooked. A brilliant idea!

Whisk the flour, sugar, baking powder, lemon zest and salt in a large bowl. Add the butter and using your fingers, rub it into the dry mixture until it resembles wet sand. Drop in the egg and bring the dough together. Tip the dough onto a well-floured work surface and lightly knead the dough and shape it into a large flat disc. Wrap in plastic wrap and set aside to rest in the fridge for 1 hour (overnight is also fine).

Preheat the oven to 180°C (350°F). Line a baking tray with baking paper.

On a well-floured work surface, roll out the dough until it is 3–4 mm (¼ in) thick. Cut out circles of dough using a 9 cm (3½ in) fluted cookie cutter. Place a heaped teaspoon of mostarda on the centre of each dough circle. Brush the edges with a bit of milk and fold over to seal, making sure you do not trap any air inside. Brush the outer surface of the raviola with a little more milk, then repeat with the remaining pastry and filling.

Bake for 15–20 minutes until the raviole are pale golden. If desired, lightly brush the surface of the raviole with a combination of bitter almond liqueur and aniseed liqueur. Sprinkle extra caster sugar over the top while they are still warm and allow to cool completely before eating.

Raviole will keep in an airtight container for up to 5 days.

MAKES 16

CANNOLI al CACAO con RICOTTA

{COCOA CANNOLI WITH RICOTTA}

GRAPESEED, PEANUT OR SUNFLOWER OIL, FOR FRYING

1 EGG WHITE, FOR BRUSHING

CRUSHED PISTACHIO NUTS, FOR GARNISH

ICING (CONFECTIONERS') SUGAR, FOR DUSTING

PASTRY

250 G (9 OZ/1²/₃ CUPS) PLAIN (ALL-PURPOSE) FLOUR

40 G (1½ OZ) CASTER (SUPERFINE) SUGAR

2 TEASPOONS GROUND CINNAMON

2 TEASPOONS DARK BITTER COCOA

2 TEASPOONS FINELY GROUND COFFEE

PINCH OF SALT

50 G (1¾ OZ) COLD UNSALTED BUTTER, CUT INTO SMALL DICE

2 TEASPOONS WHITE WINE VINEGAR

50 ML (1¾ FL OZ) DRY WHITE WINE

1 EGG, LIGHTLY BEATEN

FILLING

600 G (1 LB 5 OZ) FIRM RICOTTA (SEE PAGE 18)

150 G (5½ OZ) CASTER (SUPERFINE) SUGAR

Cannoli are one of the most popular and well-known sweet Sicilian street foods. The pastry is traditionally made with strutto (a type of pork fat), which makes the shells very crisp. This version uses butter but please feel free to substitute strutto if you know anyone who can get it for you! Although not traditional, I have added cinnamon, cocoa and coffee to the pastry just like they do at my local Sicilian restaurant. Cannoli can be filled with vanilla or chocolate custard but I love the traditional version filled with sweet ricotta and the ends dipped in chopped nuts. You will need metal cannoli tubes to make the shape, which can be purchased from most homeware shops. Alternatively, you can try using scrunched aluminium foil, but they won't be as even.

To make the pastry, place the flour, sugar, cinnamon, cocoa, coffee and salt in a large bowl. Scatter over the butter and using your fingers, work the butter into the dry ingredients until the mixture resembles breadcrumbs. Add the vinegar, wine and egg and stir until well incorporated. Tip the dough onto a lightly floured work surface and knead for about 2 minutes until smooth. Wrap in plastic wrap and set aside in the fridge for at least 1 hour.

To make the filling, combine the ricotta and sugar in a bowl until you have a smooth cream. Alternatively, you can do this in a food processor. If you have a particularly sweet tooth, feel free to add a bit of extra sugar, to taste. Set aside in the fridge until ready to use.

Roll out the pastry on a lightly floured work surface to 1–2 mm (¹⁄₁₆ in) thick. You can also use a pasta machine to roll out the dough, taking it down to the third-last setting. Cut out circles of dough using a 9 cm (3½ in) cookie cutter.

Heat plenty of oil in a small deep saucepan or deep-fryer to 170°C (340°F) or until a scrap of dough dropped into the oil bubbles immediately.

Wrap the dough circles around metal cannoli tubes so that the edges overlap slightly. Seal the two edges with egg white and press firmly. Brush a little egg white over the shell as well.

>>

CANNOLI al CACAO con RICOTTA

Cook the cannoli tubes, one at a time, for 2–2½ minutes until brown. Lift out the cannoli by holding the metal tube with heatproof tongs (or lift up the basket if using a deep-fryer). Shake the shell from the tube and place on kitchen towel to absorb any excess oil. If the shells do not come off easily, then leave the cannolo to cool slightly, then hold it gently with kitchen towel and use the tongs to lift the metal tube out from the cooked pastry. Carefully wipe the metal tube with kitchen towel and wrap another uncooked pastry circle around the tube, sealing it well with egg white. Repeat until they are all cooked.

Fill the shells with the ricotta cream, using a knife to push the mixture into the tubes from either end. Alternatively, place the sweet ricotta in a piping bag and pipe into the tubes using a wide nozzle. Dip the ends of the cannoli in crushed pistachio nuts, then dust with icing sugar and serve.

If you are not going to eat them immediately, leave the shells unfilled in an airtight container. They will keep for about 1 week.

MAKES 20–24

CROSTOLI

{ SWEET FRIED PASTRY WINGS }

650 G (1 LB 7 OZ) PLAIN (ALL-PURPOSE) FLOUR, PLUS EXTRA FOR DUSTING

85 G (3 OZ) CASTER (SUPERFINE) SUGAR

PINCH OF SALT

2 LARGE EGGS, PLUS 1 EGG YOLK, LIGHTLY BEATEN

45 ML (1½ FL OZ) GRAPPA, BRANDY OR MARSALA

ZEST OF 1 ORANGE

3 TEASPOONS WHITE WINE VINEGAR

GRAPESEED, PEANUT OR SUNFLOWER OIL, FOR FRYING

ICING (CONFECTIONERS') SUGAR, FOR DUSTING

Crostoli are known as cenci, galani, sfrappole or bugie depending on which region or town in Italy you are in, and are typically eaten at Carnevale on the days leading up to Lent. This is my mother's recipe and she swears that the secret to good crostoli is to make the pastry very thin, so that the ribbons of dough cook quickly and become crisp. I use a pasta machine to achieve this, which is not necessary but it makes your work a bit easier if you have one!

Place the flour, sugar and salt in a large bowl. Add the egg, grappa, brandy or Marsala, orange zest, vinegar and 70 ml (2¼ fl oz) water, and mix with a wooden spoon. Alternatively, mix the ingredients in a food processor. Empty onto a lightly floured work surface and knead for a few minutes until the dough is smooth, firm and homogenous. If the pastry is a little crumbly, add a little more water and knead until you have the right consistency. Wrap in plastic wrap and set aside to rest for at least 30 minutes.

Divide the dough into quarters, keeping the dough you are not working on well covered in plastic wrap. On a well-floured work surface, roll one piece of dough into a rectangular shape that will fit through the widest setting of your pasta machine. Roll the dough through the machine, then reduce the setting and keep feeding the dough through until you get to the thinnest or second thinnest setting. Roll through the last setting three times.

Using a fluted pastry wheel, cut the edges off the dough and then cut into three long thin strips. Cut each strip into 8 cm (3¼ in) pieces. Again, using the pastry wheel, make a cut in the centre of each strip, then thread one end through the cut to make a bow (you don't have to make the bow – the strips will be fine – but the bow is much prettier). Repeat with the remaining dough.

To cook, heat enough oil for deep-frying in a deep heavy-based saucepan or deep-fryer to 180°C (350°F) or until a scrap of dough sizzles immediately in the oil. Cook 3–4 crostoli at a time for about 30 seconds on one side until the edges start to colour. Turn over and cook briefly on the other side. Drain on kitchen towel and allow to cool a little before dusting with icing sugar. The crostoli will keep, without icing sugar, stored in an airtight container for several weeks.

MAKES ABOUT 80

TORCINELLI

{ POTATO FRITTERS WITH ANISEED }

1 LARGE OR 2 SMALL DESIREE POTATOES (YOU WILL NEED 175 G/6 OZ COOKED POTATO)

175 G (6 OZ) PLAIN (ALL-PURPOSE) FLOUR

1 TEASPOON INSTANT DRIED YEAST

40 G (1¼ OZ) CASTER (SUPERFINE) SUGAR, PLUS EXTRA FOR DUSTING

30 ML (1 FL OZ) TEPID MILK

1 EGG

40 G (1¼ OZ/⅓ CUP) SULTANAS (GOLDEN RAISINS), SOAKED IN WARM WATER FOR 10 MINUTES

½ TEASPOON ANISEED (OR SUBSTITUTE ¼ TEASPOON CRUSHED STAR ANISE OR ¾ TEASPOON FENNEL SEEDS)

PINCH OF SALT

GRAPESEED OIL OR PEANUT OIL, FOR FRYING

LIGHT OLIVE OIL (TO HELP ROLL OUT THE DOUGH)

GROUND CINNAMON, FOR DUSTING

You find vegetables in the most unexpected places – like potatoes in these sweet fried Abruzzese delights. Torcinelli are traditionally eaten around Easter, but in the pasticceria where I bought them in Pescara, I was told they are popular all year round. They were freshly made, still warm, covered in granulated sugar and unexpectedly light. The addition of aniseed gives them a lovely warming taste.

Scrub the potato and place in a small saucepan of salted water and bring to the boil. Simmer, covered, for about 30 minutes or until tender. Drain, peel and mash (or push through a potato ricer), and keep warm.

Place the flour, yeast and sugar in a bowl and lightly whisk to combine. Add the warm mashed potato, milk and egg, and give the mixture a good stir with a wooden spoon for at least 5 minutes, until the mixture is homogenous and smooth. Alternatively, use a stand mixer.

Drain the sultanas, making sure you squeeze out the excess liquid, then add them to the mixture along with the aniseed and salt. Give it a good final stir – the dough will be quite soft. Cover with plastic wrap and set aside in a warm place for about 1 hour or until doubled in size.

Heat enough oil for deep-frying in a heavy-based saucepan or deep-fryer to 180°C (350°F). With well-oiled hands, take 1 heaped tablespoon of dough and roll into a short baton, then twist to form the traditional shape. Repeat with the remaining dough.

Cook 3–4 torcinelli at a time for 2–3 minutes on each side until pale golden all over and cooked through. Break open the first torcinello to check it is cooked and adjust the temperature of the oil, if necessary, before proceeding with the remaining torcinelli.

Drain on kitchen towel, then transfer to a bowl and toss in the extra sugar while still warm. Sprinkle over a little ground cinnamon just before serving.

The torcinelli are best eaten on the day they are made.

MAKES APPROXIMATELY 15

TARALLI al LIMONE

{LEMON TARALLI}

TARALLI

250 G (9 OZ/1²/₃ OZ) PLAIN (ALL-PURPOSE) FLOUR
50 G (1¾ OZ) CORNFLOUR (CORNSTARCH)
1 SCANT TEASPOON BAKING POWDER
PINCH OF SALT
100 G (3½ OZ) CASTER (SUPERFINE) SUGAR
ZEST OF 1 LEMON
90 G (3 OZ) COLD UNSALTED BUTTER, DICED
2 EGGS, LIGHTLY BEATEN

ICING

150 G (5½ OZ) ICING (CONFECTIONERS') SUGAR
30 ML (1 FL OZ) FRESHLY SQUEEZED LEMON JUICE

These soft, sweet, ring-shaped taralli are typical of Sicily, in particular Palermo. They are fragrant and lemony, with citrus zest in the tarallo and lemon juice in the icing. I like to rub the lemon zest into the sugar with my fingertips – it seems to make the taralli even more lemony.

Place the flours, baking powder and salt in a bowl and lightly whisk until combined.

Place the sugar and lemon zest in another bowl and using the tips of your fingers, rub the zest into the sugar until it is well incorporated. Add this mixture to the dry ingredients and whisk lightly.

Again, using your fingertips, work the butter into the dry ingredients until it has a sandy texture. Drop in the egg and mix with a wooden spoon until well combined. Using your hands, bring the mixture together and knead briefly until it is homogenous and smooth. Wrap in plastic wrap and set aside in the fridge for 1 hour.

Preheat the oven to 170°C (340°F).

Divide the dough into 30 g (1 oz) balls, then roll each ball into a small sausage and join the two ends to make a slightly overlapping ring. Bake for 25 minutes or until pale golden, then transfer to a wire rack to cool.

To make the icing, place the icing sugar and lemon juice in a bowl and whisk vigorously until the icing is smooth. Dip the top of the cooled taralli into the icing then place on a wire rack until the icing hardens.

The taralli will keep in an airtight container for 3–4 days.

MAKES APPROXIMATELY 18

PARDULE

{ SARDINIAN RICOTTA CAKES }

RICOTTA FILLING

300 G (10½ OZ) RICOTTA (SEE PAGE 18)

35 G (1¼ OZ) CASTER (SUPERFINE) SUGAR

30 G (1 OZ) PLAIN (ALL-PURPOSE) FLOUR

1 EGG, PLUS 1 EGG YOLK

ZEST OF ½ LARGE ORANGE

ZEST OF ½ LARGE LEMON

½ TEASPOON BAKING POWDER

PINCH OF SAFFRON (OR ½ TEASPOON PURE VANILLA ESSENCE)

DOUGH

150 G (5½ OZ) FINE SEMOLINA

2 TEASPOONS CASTER (SUPERFINE) SUGAR

20 G (¾ OZ) BUTTER, CUBED

PLAIN (ALL-PURPOSE) FLOUR, FOR DUSTING

BRUSHING

2 TABLESPOONS WARMED HONEY, MIXED WITH 1 TABLESPOON HOT WATER

Saffron-scented honey-brushed ricotta pastries are typical of Sardinia. They are typically made with fresh sheep's milk ricotta and have a star-shaped appearance. The dough is bread-like and not sweet, although I prefer to add just a bit of sugar to it. I found these in a market on the outskirts of Rome, where the locals were queuing to buy a pardula to enjoy as they roamed the markets.

To make the ricotta filling, place the ricotta in a bowl and whisk for several minutes until the ricotta is super smooth. Add the sugar, flour, eggs, zests, baking powder and saffron and whisk until smooth. Set the filing aside while you make the dough.

Place the semolina and caster sugar on a clean work surface and make a well in the centre. Drop in the butter and work it through the semolina using your fingertips until it resembles fine breadcrumbs. Add 30 ml (1 fl oz) water and work it through the dough. Drizzle in another 30 ml (1 fl oz) water, a little at a time, until the dough is smooth and pliable. Divide into two and set half aside.

On a lightly floured work surface, roll the dough half into a rectangle, then put it through the widest setting of a pasta machine. Reduce the setting, then roll it through again, repeating and making it thinner each time until you reach the middle setting. Cut out circles of dough using a 9 cm (3½ in) cookie cutter, re-rolling any scraps to make more circles. Repeat with the remaining dough. You should have 14–15 circles in total.

Preheat the oven to 180°C (350°F). Line a baking tray with baking paper.

Place a heaped tablespoon of ricotta filling in the centre of each circle, leaving a 1 cm (½ in) border. Pinch the dough on either side of the circle using your thumb and forefinger, then repeat at intervals around the circle until you have six points. Flatten the ricotta with your finger or the back of a spoon and place on the prepared baking tray. Repeat with the remaining dough and filling.

Bake for 30–35 minutes until the ricotta is pale golden and cooked through. Set aside to cool on a wire rack and brush with the honey and water. Eat warm or at room temperature. Pardule will keep in an airtight container in the fridge for 2 days.

MAKES ABOUT 15

CASTAGNOLE di RICOTTA

{ SWEET RICOTTA BALLS }

80 G (2¾) RICOTTA

25 G (1OZ) CASTER (SUPERFINE) SUGAR, PLUS EXTRA FOR DUSTING

1 EGG

ZEST OF ½ LEMON

ZEST OF ½ ORANGE

½ TEASPOON SWEET MARSALA (OR OTHER SWEET WINE)

150 G (5½ OZ/1 CUP) 00 WEAK (CAKE) FLOUR (SEE PAGE 17), PLUS EXTRA FOR DUSTING

1 TEASPOON BAKING POWDER

PINCH OF SALT

20 ML (¾ FL OZ) FULL-CREAM (WHOLE) MILK

GRAPESEED, PEANUT OR SUNFLOWER OIL, FOR FRYING

Castagnole get their name from their size – castagne means chestnuts. They are delightful balls of sweet ricotta, fried and then dusted with sugar. They are sometimes called favette (meaning little kidney-shaped beans) and are found in many regions of Italy, from north to south. They can be made with or without ricotta and can also be baked, but I love the fried version, made with sweet Marsala, lemon and orange zest.

Combine the ricotta and sugar in a small bowl and mix with a fork. Add the egg and continue to mix until smooth. Add the zests and Marsala and mix well.

In a separate bowl, whisk together the flour, baking powder and salt, then tip into the ricotta mixture and incorporate with a wooden spoon. When the mixture starts to clump together, add half the milk, mix and then add the rest of the milk. Stir, until well combined. Alternatively, you can prepare the mixture in a stand mixer set to low speed.

Tip the dough onto a floured work surface. The dough should be quite sticky but cohesive. Knead gently until it forms a smooth ball. Transfer the dough to a bowl, cover with a clean tea towel and set aside to rest for 1 hour–1 hour 15 minutes. The longer you rest it, the lighter the ricotta balls will be.

Cut the dough in half, then roll each half into a long rope. Cut each rope into 10 equal-sized pieces and roll into balls. You should get at least 20.

Heat at least 5 cm (2 in) of oil in a small deep saucepan or deep-fryer to 180°C (350°F) or until a cube of bread dropped into the oil sizzles in 5 seconds. Cook the castagnole in batches for 3–4 minutes until pale golden all over. If the heat is too high, they will be too dark on the outside and raw on the inside. Cut open the first castagnole to check it is cooked and adjust the oil temperature if necessary. Drain on kitchen towel and sprinkle with caster sugar while they are still hot.

Eat warm and if they have cooled down, reheat for about 10 seconds in a microwave oven. Castagnole are best eaten on the day they are made.

MAKES 20–24

iL GELATA

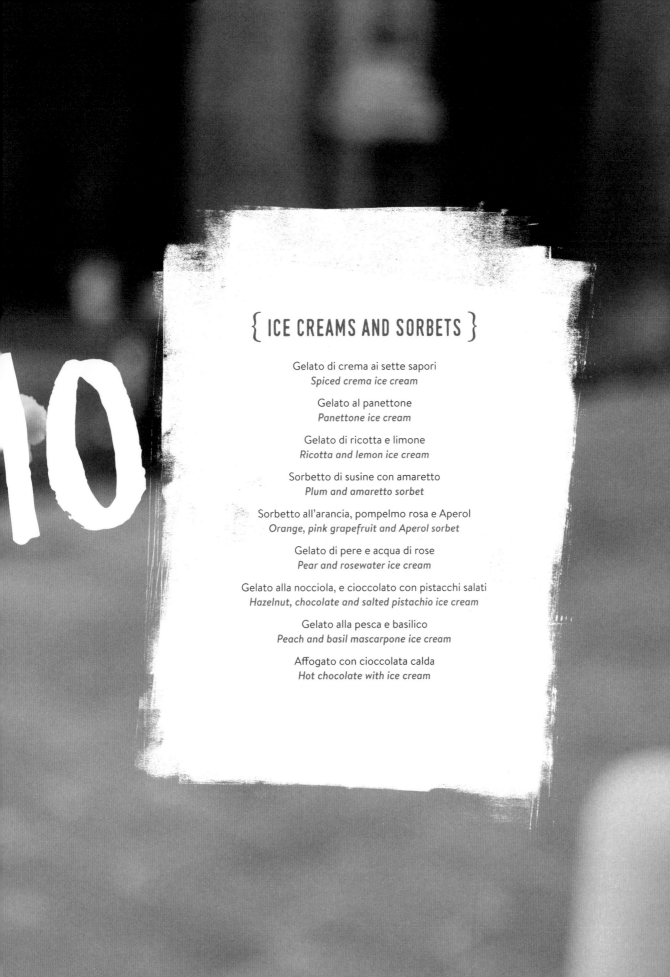

{ ICE CREAMS AND SORBETS }

Gelato di crema ai sette sapori
Spiced crema ice cream

Gelato al panettone
Panettone ice cream

Gelato di ricotta e limone
Ricotta and lemon ice cream

Sorbetto di susine con amaretto
Plum and amaretto sorbet

Sorbetto all'arancia, pompelmo rosa e Aperol
Orange, pink grapefruit and Aperol sorbet

Gelato di pere e acqua di rose
Pear and rosewater ice cream

Gelato alla nocciola, e cioccolato con pistacchi salati
Hazelnut, chocolate and salted pistachio ice cream

Gelato alla pesca e basilico
Peach and basil mascarpone ice cream

Affogato con cioccolata calda
Hot chocolate with ice cream

Nothing is sweeter than going for an afternoon or early evening pre-dinner stroll to buy gelato, then walking through the piazza eating it from a cone, or from a cup with a spoon. The season doesn't seem to matter that much either, in particular to tourists, as ice creams are consumed almost as much in winter as they are in summer. It is the ultimate sweet street food, loved by all.

Ice cream dates back to 1500s Europe and was first made with shaved ice and fruit juices, resulting in *sorbetti* (sorbets) rather than creamy gelato. Continued experimentation meant cream was added, then eggs, and in the mid-1800s a hand-cranked machine was invented that churned the liquid part of the ice cream while simultaneously freezing it. This resulted in a smoother, less granular ice cream, similar to the gelato we know today. In the late 1800s, *carretti del gelato* (ice-cream carts), either hand-drawn, bicycle-drawn or horse-drawn became popular throughout Europe (as well as in the USA), and once the motor vehicle was invented, ice-cream trucks rather than carts became the norm.

In Italy, you will find gelato for sale on almost every street corner. At fairs and markets, you might find a carretto, which are gaining renewed popularity, often attached to a Piaggio Ape (pronounced *ah-peah*), a 3-wheeled driveable vehicle that's a little like a Vespa.

The gelataio not only makes the ice cream, coming up with new and different flavours, but also drives the cart and serves customers. And these days, they may well be university trained. Carpignani is a Gelato University located in Bologna in central Italy. It provides advanced courses and internships in gelato-making, in many languages, as well as being connected to a gelato museum. They strive to achieve 'gelato excellence' and if the number of artisan gelatai around is any indication, they are certainly succeeding in achieving that goal.

The fact that there are so many *gelaterie* (ice-cream shops) can make it tricky for the tourist to find the best and most authentic ice cream – look for signs that say 'artisan' or 'made with whole milk'. Also check the flavours – they should be seasonal (do not expect to have an authentic peach ice cream in winter). The colour may be another giveaway – something that looks fake might be just that. If in doubt, there are many online blogs and websites showcasing the best gelato available in any given area.

GELATO di CREMA ai SETTE SAPORI

{ SPICED CREMA ICE CREAM }

375 ML (12½ FL OZ/1½ CUPS) FULL-CREAM (WHOLE) MILK

150 G (5½ OZ) SUGAR

PINCH OF SALT

375 ML (12½ FL OZ/1½ CUPS) THICK (DOUBLE/HEAVY) CREAM

PEEL FROM ½ SMALL ORANGE, WHITE PITH REMOVED

PEEL FROM ½ LEMON, WHITE PITH REMOVED

8 WHOLE CLOVES

1½ CINNAMON STICKS

20 G (¾ OZ) COFFEE BEANS

5–6 WHOLE STAR ANISE

½ VANILLA BEAN, SEEDS SCRAPED

5 EGG YOLKS

It was the depths of winter on my last trip to Italy, but that didn't stop me from eating gelato most days. Winter is a time when creamy spice-infused gelato seems particularly appropriate. This recipe is inspired by a gelato I had in Florence, from a tiny gelataria oltr'Arno (on the other side of the Arno river, which divides the city in two) on a particularly cold day. It is not only infused with spices and citrus rind but also coffee beans. It is best infused overnight for maximum flavour.

Place the milk, sugar, salt, 125 ml (4 fl oz/½ cup) of the cream, orange and lemon peel, cloves, cinnamon sticks, coffee beans, star anise and vanilla bean and seeds in a medium-sized saucepan over medium heat. Heat until warm, but do not allow the mixture to boil. Remove from the heat, cover and allow to infuse in the fridge for 8 hours or, preferably, overnight.

Whisk the egg yolks in a large bowl and set aside.

Place the remaining cream in a large bowl and set a large strainer over the top. Sit the bowl in an ice bath.

Strain the chilled milk and cream mixture into a medium-sized saucepan and warm through over medium heat. Do not allow the mixture to boil. Remove from the heat and slowly pour into the beaten egg, stirring constantly with a wooden spoon to prevent the egg from scrambling. Scrape the mixture back into the saucepan and keep stirring over low heat until the mixture starts to thicken and coat the back of the spoon. Pour through the strainer into the bowl of cream and stir until completely cool.

Pour the mixture into your ice-cream machine and churn according to the manufacturer's instructions. Freeze for about 1 hour before serving.

If the ice cream has been in the freezer overnight, take it out about 10 minutes before serving.

MAKES ABOUT 1 LITRE (34 FL OZ/4 CUPS)

GELATO al PANETTONE

{ PANETTONE ICE CREAM }

375 ML (12½ FL OZ/1½ CUPS) FULL-CREAM (WHOLE) MILK

100 G (3½ OZ) SUGAR

PINCH OF SALT

375 ML (12½ FL OZ/1½ CUPS) THICK (DOUBLE/HEAVY) CREAM

100 G (3½ OZ) DRIED DATES, ROUGHLY CHOPPED

PEEL FROM 2 MEDIUM–LARGE ORANGES, WHITE PITH REMOVED

LARGE PINCH OF SAFFRON

¼ VANILLA BEAN, SEEDS SCRAPED (OR ¼ TEASPOON VANILLA BEAN PASTE)

5 EGG YOLKS

25 G (1 OZ) ORANGE-BLOSSOM HONEY

25 G (1 OZ) SULTANAS (GOLDEN RAISINS)

40 ML (1½ FL OZ) SWEET MARSALA

Gelato al panettone was a popular new flavour when I was last in Italy. Many gelati shops had a sign with 'panettone' written on it. After eating it a couple of times, I noted that it didn't seem to be made with actual panettone but with the flavours for which panettone is best known. So, after some experimenting at home and an evening of gelato-testing with some foodie friends from Umbria, I came up with my own recipe.

Place the milk, sugar, salt, 125 ml (4 fl oz/½ cup) of the cream, dates, orange peel, saffron threads and vanilla bean and seeds in a medium-sized saucepan over medium heat. Heat until warm, but do not allow the mixture to boil. Remove from the heat, cover and allow to infuse in the fridge for 8 hours or, preferably, overnight.

Whisk the egg yolks in a large bowl and set aside.

Place the remaining cream in a large bowl and set a large strainer over the top. Sit the bowl in an ice bath.

Strain the chilled milk and cream mixture into a saucepan and add the honey. Warm through over medium heat and stir until the honey dissolves. Do not allow the mixture to boil. Slowly pour the mixture onto the egg yolks, whisking the whole time. Scrape the mixture back into the pan over medium heat, stirring the whole time with a wooden spoon. Heat until the mixture starts to thicken and coat the back of the spoon. Pour through the strainer into the bowl of cream and stir until completely cool.

Soak the sultanas in the Marsala for at least 15 minutes.

Pour the cooled cream mixture into an ice-cream machine and churn according to the manufacturer's instructions. When ready, drain and roughly chop the sultanas, then fold through the churned ice cream. You can also stir through some of the remaining liquor, if you like. Freeze for about 1 hour (or 3 hours if you have stirred through the liquor) before serving.

If the ice cream has been in the freezer overnight, take it out about 10 minutes before serving.

MAKES ABOUT 1 LITRE (34 FL OZ/4 CUPS)

GELATO di RICOTTA e LIMONE

{ RICOTTA AND LEMON ICE CREAM }

100 ML (3½ FL OZ) FULL-CREAM (WHOLE) MILK

180 G (6½ OZ) SUGAR

250 G (9 OZ) RICOTTA (THE FRESHEST YOU CAN FIND) (SEE PAGE 18)

PEEL FROM 1 LEMON, WHITE PITH REMOVED

250 ML (8½ FL OZ/1 CUP) POURING (SINGLE/LIGHT) CREAM

ZEST OF 1 LEMON

I first ate ricotta gelato in Sicily. As ricotta is one of my favourite ingredients to use in the kitchen, I knew that I was likely to love it. And it bowled me over. The ricotta was no doubt made from sheep's milk and very fresh. As this is quite difficult to buy in a big city, I decided to pair it with lemon in this recipe. To make it extra citrusy, lemon is not only added initially, as an infusion, but also at the end after the gelato has been churned. It tastes like an Italian lemon ricotta cheesecake filling. It is made without eggs, so it is quicker to make than a custard-based gelato.

Place the milk and sugar in a medium-sized bowl. Using a stick blender (ideally with a whisk attachment if you have one), mix the milk and sugar then add the ricotta – about 50 g (1¾ oz) at a time – making sure it is incorporated and smooth before adding the next piece. Add the lemon peel, cover with plastic wrap and set aside in the fridge for at least 3 hours or overnight.

Remove the lemon peel and stir through the cream. Pour into an ice-cream machine and churn for about 30 minutes until firm. Stir as much of the lemon zest as you like through the prepared gelato.

Place in an airtight container and freeze for a few hours before eating.

MAKES ABOUT 1 LITRE (34 FL OZ/4 CUPS)

SORBETTO di SUSINE con AMARETTO

{ PLUM AND AMARETTO SORBET }

230 G (8 OZ/1 CUP) CASTER (SUPERFINE) SUGAR

½ VANILLA BEAN (OR ½ TEASPOON VANILLA BEAN PASTE)

800 G (1 LB 12 OZ) LARGE RIPE BLOOD OR MARIPOSA RED PLUMS, STONED AND ROUGHLY CHOPPED

2 TEASPOONS LEMON JUICE

2 TABLESPOONS AMARETTO (OR MORE OR LESS, TO TASTE)

My family in Italy live close to the seaside town of Grado, which is hugely popular with Austrian and German tourists as well as Italians. Every time I visit, I go back to the same gelataria and sample the new flavours. The last time I was there in summer I had a plum sorbet, which was very seasonal and very refreshing. I love the combination of plums and almonds so have added a splash of amaretto to the final churn.

Dissolve the sugar in 250 ml (8½ fl oz/1 cup) water in a small saucepan over medium heat. Transfer to a heatproof jug and add the vanilla bean. Set aside in the fridge for at least 3 hours for the water to chill and the vanilla bean to infuse. When ready, remove the vanilla bean and dry for another use.

Heat the plums in a medium-sized saucepan over low heat until the plums soften. Set aside to cool a little, then slip the skins off.

Place the plum pulp in a food processor and pulse until smooth (it may be quite liquidy). You want to have about 650 g (1 lb 7 oz) of plum pulp. Transfer to a bowl and set aside in the fridge to chill for a couple of hours.

Place an airtight container in the freezer to chill.

Combine the plums with 300 ml (10 fl oz) of the sugar syrup and add the lemon juice. Pour into an ice-cream machine and churn according to the manufacturer's instructions. If the mixture is well chilled beforehand, it should churn to the right consistency in about 45 minutes. Pour in the amaretto (as much or as little as desired – or you can even omit it) and give it a final churn.

Transfer the sorbet to the chilled container and place in the freezer. The alcohol increases the freezing temperature so it will take a little longer to set. Chill for at least 2 hours before serving.

If you leave it overnight to freeze, remove from the freezer 10–15 minutes before serving.

MAKES ABOUT 1 LITRE (34 FL OZ/4 CUPS)

SORBETTO ALL'ARANCIA, POMPELMO ROSA e APEROL

{ ORANGE, PINK GRAPEFRUIT AND APEROL SORBET }

100 ML (3½ FL OZ) FRESHLY SQUEEZED PINK GRAPEFRUIT JUICE (ABOUT 1 LARGE GRAPEFRUIT)

400 ML (13½ FL OZ) FRESHLY SQUEEZED ORANGE JUICE (ABOUT 4 ORANGES)

80 G (2¾ OZ) SUGAR

80 ML (2½ FL OZ/⅓ CUP) APEROL

Aperol is very well known nowadays because of the Aperol Spritz, which marries it with sparkling Prosecco. It also makes a summery sorbet with freshly squeezed orange juice and pink grapefruit juice, giving it a slightly bitter but refreshing taste.

Place the grapefruit juice, 100ml (3½ fl oz) of the orange juice and the sugar in a small saucepan. Place over medium heat and stir until the sugar is dissolved. Add the remaining orange juice and Aperol and stir before transferring to a jug and placing in the fridge to chill completely.

Transfer to an ice-cream machine and churn according to the manufacturer's instructions. Place in an airtight container and place in the freezer for 2 hours before serving.

Remove from the freezer 5–10 minutes before serving.

MAKES ABOUT 1 LITRE (34 FL OZ/4 CUPS)

GELATO di PERE e ACQUA di ROSE

{ PEAR AND ROSEWATER ICE CREAM }

3 RIPE BEURRE BOSC PEARS, PEELED, CORED AND THINLY SLICED

2 TEASPOONS LEMON JUICE

130 G (4½ OZ) CASTER (SUPERFINE) SUGAR

250 ML (8½ FL OZ/1 CUP) THICK (DOUBLE/HEAVY) CREAM

125 ML (4 FL OZ/½ CUP) FULL-CREAM (WHOLE) MILK

20 ML (¾ FL OZ) ROSEWATER

GOOD PINCH OF SALT

Rosewater isn't an ingredient you traditionally associate with Italian food, but these days, where the boundaries between different cultures blur, it is occasionally found in cakes and desserts. I found a gelato with rosewater in Venice – it was fragrant, delicate and very refreshing. In this recipe, I have matched it with sweet ripe pears, which balances the floral taste beautifully.

Place the pear in a ceramic dish, drizzle over the lemon juice and cook in the microwave for about 2 minutes until soft. Alternatively place in a medium-sized saucepan and cook over medium heat until cooked through. Drain off the excess juice (you should have about 300 g/10½ oz of pear pulp), stir in the sugar and then blitz in a food processor until puréed. Cover with plastic wrap and set aside in the fridge for 2 hours until completely chilled.

Add the cream, milk, rosewater and salt to the pear and mix well to combine. Pour into an ice-cream machine and churn according to the manufacturer's instructions.

Transfer to an airtight container and freeze for a few hours.

If serving the gelato the following day, remove from the freezer 20 minutes before serving.

This gelato is best eaten within 3–4 days.

MAKES ABOUT 1 LITRE (34 FL OZ/4 CUPS)

GELATO alla NOCCIOLA, e CIOCCOLATO con PISTACCHI SALATI

{ HAZELNUT, CHOCOLATE AND SALTED PISTACHIO ICE CREAM }

200 G (7 OZ) HAZELNUTS, ROASTED AND SKINS REMOVED

375 ML (12½ FL OZ/1½ CUPS) FULL-CREAM (WHOLE) MILK

150 G (5½ OZ/¾ CUP) SUGAR

PINCH OF SALT

375 ML (12½ FL OZ/1½ CUPS) THICKENED (DOUBLE/HEAVY)CREAM

100 G (3½ OZ) MILK CHOCOLATE, FINELY CHOPPED

¼ TEASPOON VANILLA ESSENCE

5 EGG YOLKS

PISTACHIO SWIRL

75 G (2¾ OZ) PISTACHIOS, SHELLED

PINCH OF SEA SALT

1 TABLESPOON HONEY

Hazelnuts and chocolate are a match made in heaven and together they form the basis for a very popular Italian spread that was traditionally eaten on bread but is now found in doughnuts and pancakes practically everywhere. My niece Chiara told me about a version she ate in a gelataria in Venice last year that had salted pistachio swirled through it. She said it was the best ice cream she had eaten on the trip. It sounded so impressive that I tried to recreate it. I love the contrast of tastes as well as the texture.

Preheat the oven to 180°C (350°F). Place the hazelnuts on a baking tray and roast for 12 minutes. Tip onto a clean tea towel and rub the skins off. Transfer the hazelnuts to a food processor and whizz until finely chopped.

Place the milk, sugar and a pinch of salt in a medium-sized saucepan over medium heat and stir until dissolved. Do not allow the mixture to boil. Add the chopped hazelnuts and transfer to a heatproof bowl. Set aside in the fridge to infuse for a few hours or, preferably, overnight.

Heat the cream in a small saucepan until just before boiling point. Place the chocolate in a large heatproof bowl and pour the cream over the chocolate. Stir gently until the chocolate has melted, then add the vanilla. Set a large strainer over the bowl and place the bowl in an ice bath.

Lightly whisk the egg yolks in a large bowl and set aside.

Strain the chilled milk mixture into a small saucepan. Warm through the milk then slowly pour into the egg yolk, whisking gently the whole time to prevent the egg scrambling. Pour the lot back into the saucepan and cook over medium heat, stirring constantly with a wooden spoon, until the mixture starts to thicken and coat the back of the spoon. Pour through the strainer into the bowl of chocolate cream and stir until completely cool.

Pour the mixture into an ice-cream machine and churn according to the manufacturer's instructions.

>>

GELATO alla NOCCIOLA, e CIOCCOLATO con PISTACCHI SALATI

To make the pistachio swirl, place the nuts in a food processor and process to a fine crumb. Add the salt and honey, pulsing until they are evenly mixed through the pistachios. Taste and make sure the salt and sweetness is well balanced, then add 2-3 tablespoons water, a little at a time, pulsing between additions until you have a thick but pourable consistency.

Transfer one-third of the ice cream to an airtight container. Using a teaspoon, swirl through one-third of the pistachio mixture. Repeat until you have used all of the ingredients, then freeze the gelato for a few hours before serving.

If serving the gelato the following day, remove from the freezer 20 minutes before serving.

MAKES ABOUT 1 LITRE (34 FL OZ/4 CUPS)

GELATO alla PESCA e BASILICO

{PEACH AND BASIL ICE CREAM}

3 LARGE RIPE WHITE PEACHES, STONED AND CUT INTO 1 CM (½ IN) DICE

200 G (7 OZ) SUGAR

25 ML (¾ FL OZ) LEMON JUICE

15 FRESH BASIL LEAVES, STALKS REMOVED, ROUGHLY TORN

½ TEASPOON VANILLA BEAN PASTE

150 ML (5 FL OZ) THICK (DOUBLE/HEAVY) CREAM

100 G (3½ OZ) MASCARPONE

PINCH OF SEA SALT

I first tasted peach and basil gelato back in 2003 when I visited Italy with my (then) young daughter. It was quite the sensation at the time, marrying herbs and fruit in a creamy gelato, which may not seem quite as unusual now. I have used ripe white peaches in this late summer recipe, making it a special ice cream that can only be made for a month or so in the year. I added vanilla bean paste to the recipe as well as a pinch of salt, which (surprising as it may sound) balanced the basil and peach beautifully. Serve this with cooled roasted peaches for an even bigger peach punch. As it contains fresh fruit and herbs, it is best eaten within three days of making.

Place the peach in a ceramic dish and sprinkle over the sugar and lemon juice, giving it a good stir until mixed through. Cover and set aside at room temperature for 3–4 hours.

Place the peach in a food processor with the torn basil leaves, vanilla bean paste, cream, mascarpone and salt. Pulse a few times until combined, but so you can still see flecks of peach skin and basil leaves. Transfer to an ice-cream machine and churn according to the manufacturer's instructions.

Place in an airtight container and freeze for a few hours.

If serving the gelato the following day, remove from the freezer 20 minutes before serving.

MAKES ABOUT 1 LITRE (34 FL OZ/4 CUPS)

AFFOGATO con CIOCCOLATA CALDA

{ Hot chocolate with ice cream }

600 ML (20½ FL OZ) FULL-CREAM (WHOLE) MILK

4 HEAPED TEASPOONS POTATO FLOUR

2 TABLESPOONS DUTCH (UNSWEETENED) COCOA POWDER

2 TABLESPOONS CASTER (SUPERFINE) SUGAR, OR TO TASTE

2 SCOOPS OF YOUR FAVOURITE ICE CREAM

To me, an affogato has always been a ball of ice cream plunged into a cup of hot coffee, (affogare means to drown). However, when I was last in Venice, the local gelataria was selling affogato. As it was December and the depths of winter, it seemed like a great idea – except at the gelataria they were making it with a thick hot chocolate, the type you commonly find in bars in Italy. A paper cup was filled three-quarters full with hot chocolate and a scoop of your choice of gelato was added. You could use the Spiced crema gelato (page 230) or your favourite vanilla ice cream.

Place the milk, potato flour, cocoa powder and sugar in a small saucepan over medium heat. Whisk until the dry ingredients dissolve and there are no lumps. Continue whisking until the milk comes to the boil and it starts to thicken. Pour into mugs and serve immediately, dropping a ball of ice cream in the mugs at the table.

MAKES 2

{ SAUCES AND BASICS }

Maionnese al limone
Lemon mayonnaise

Maionnese all'aglio
Garlic mayonnaise

Brodo di carne
Beef stock

Salsa di pomodoro
Simple tomato salsa

Salsa di pomodoro e piselli
Pea and tomato salsa

Il sugo di Livia
Livia's meat sugo

A book on street food wouldn't be complete without nonna's recipes, as nonna's kitchen is where the knowledge of food starts. She is the traditional much-loved centre of family meals, standing over the kitchen stove, stirring a pot of fragrant meat sugo. She is an integral and essential part of the kitchen, full of practical cooking wisdom and stories learned from watching her nonna cook over the same *fogolar* (hearth).

She knows the recipes by heart, as she has been making them for so many years. All cups and spoons are not standard and when you ask her how much you should add of this ingredient or that spice, she will reply '*quanto basta*' (as much as you need). This makes it a little difficult to write the recipes down on paper, and this is probably the way she intended it to be. You need to know the food, understand the consistency and tastes, and then you will work it out by feel – not the easiest thing to do when you are learning a new cuisine or starting out on your cooking journey. The best thing to do if you do not have a nonna, is find someone else's nonna, and follow her around the kitchen for a couple of days, with a camera, a piece of paper, a pair of able hands and a good appetite.

As nonna is a key inspiration and imparter of food stories and memories, it is here that you will find recipes for sauces that go with or are a fundamental part of some of the dishes in this book. The barista, friggitore, fornaio and pasticciere all probably first learned about food in nonna's kitchen, rushing home from school to a hot bowl of pasta and salsa di pomodoro, or helping nonna make panzerotti or crostoli.

MAIONNESE al LIMONE

{ LEMON MAYONNAISE }

1 EGG YOLK
½ TEASPOON WHITE WINE VINEGAR
½ TEASPOON LEMON JUICE (OPTIONAL)
125 ML (4 FL OZ/½ CUP) VEGETABLE OIL
FINELY GRATED ZEST OF ½ LEMON

Lemon mayonnaise goes with all sorts of seafood, and is especially delicious served with Fritto misto di pesce in cono (page 130), and Cozze fritte (page 129). You can also stir lemon juice and/or zest into store-bought mayonnaise, but it is so easy to make your own. If you like mustard in your mayonnaise, add ½ teaspoon at the same time as the vinegar.

Place the egg yolk, vinegar and lemon juice (if using) in a medium-sized bowl with high sides. Whisk briefly with an electric or hand-held whisk to break the yolk. Continue to whisk vigorously and slowly drizzle in the oil in a steady stream – it should take almost a minute to add. The mixture will thicken and turn into mayonnaise. Stir through the lemon zest and season with salt, to taste.

This mayonnaise is best eaten within 24 hours of making it.

MAKES ABOUT 125 ML (4 FL OZ/½ CUP)

MAIONNESE ALL'AGLIO

{ GARLIC MAYONNAISE }

2 GARLIC CLOVES, UNPEELED
¼ TEASPOON OLIVE OIL
1 EGG YOLK
½ TEASPOON WHITE WINE VINEGAR
125 ML (4 FL OZ/½ CUP) VEGETABLE OIL

Unlike French mayonnaise, Italian mayonnaise is generally made without mustard. However, if you like the taste of mustard, you can add 1/2 teaspoon at the same time as the vinegar and adjust the amount of salt. Adding roasted garlic makes this mayonnaise particularly delicious and well-suited to Polpette di sarde (page 120).

Preheat the oven to 180°C (350°F). Line a small baking tray with baking paper.

Rub the garlic cloves with the olive oil and place them on the baking tray. Roast for 15 minutes or until soft. Squeeze the garlic out of their skins and transfer to a medium-sized bowl.

Add the egg yolk and vinegar, and whisk briefly with an electric or hand-held whisk to break the yolk. Continue to whisk vigorously and slowly drizzle in the oil in a steady stream – it should take almost a minute to add. The mixture will thicken and turn into mayonnaise. Season with salt, to taste.

This mayonnaise is best eaten within 24 hours of making it.

MAKES ABOUT 125 ML (4 FL OZ/½ CUP)

BRODO di CARNE

{ BEEF STOCK }

800 G (1 LB 12 OZ) BEEF IN A SINGLE PIECE (ASK YOUR BUTCHER FOR THE BEST CUT FOR MAKING BROTH)

PIECE OF BEEF BONE

1 MEDIUM CARROT, ROUGHLY CHOPPED

1 CELERY STALK, ROUGHLY CHOPPED

½ SMALL WHITE ONION, PEELED AND BASE REMOVED

A FEW PARSLEY SPRIGS

I usually use a sinewy, yet flavoursome cut of beef to make beef stock so that it will withstand a couple of hours simmering. I also ask my butcher for a bone and throw that in for good measure. The beef can be used after simmering in dishes such as bollito misto (mixed boiled meats), and to make Panino con lesso alla picchiapò (page 108), in which the meat is added to a tomato-based sauce and used to make a deliciously tender and typically Roman dish that can be served with mashed potatoes, or in a rosetta roll for lunch on the go.

Place all of the ingredients in a large heavy-based stockpot and cover with water. Bring to the boil, then cover and reduce the heat to low and simmer for about 2 hours. You can also use a pressure cooker for 45 minutes on high, then slowly release the pressure. Remove from the heat and set aside to cool.

Strain the broth into a large bowl, cover with plastic wrap and place in the fridge overnight. (Chilling the broth allows the fat to settle and rise to the surface. You can then scoop it off quite easily and strain the broth through some muslin/cheesecloth to remove any remaining impurities.)

Pick out the meat from the leftover ingredients to use in other dishes or just eat as is, thinly sliced with a bit of sea salt.

If you are going to use the broth in the next 3–4 days, keep it in the fridge. Otherwise, decant into small airtight containers and place in the freezer to use over the next few months.

MAKES ABOUT 2 LITRES (68 FL OZ/8 CUPS)

SALSA di POMODORO

{ SIMPLE TOMATO SALSA }

400 G (14 OZ) TINNED PEELED ROMA TOMATOES
30 G (1 OZ) UNSALTED BUTTER
½ MEDIUM BROWN ONION, PEELED
PINCH OF SUGAR

*This recipe is inspired by a classic Marcela Hazan dish. I make it every week
as it goes with everything, from a dipping sauce to a midweek plate of pasta.*

Place all of the ingredients in a small saucepan, breaking up the tomatoes with
a wooden spoon. Cover and simmer over low heat for 30–40 minutes, until a layer
of oil separates from the tomatoes and the sauce has thickened. Season with salt,
to taste.

Remove the onion and, if you like, whizz the sauce with a stick blender.

The salsa will keep in a ceramic or glass container, covered, in the fridge for up
to 3 days.

MAKES ABOUT 375 ML (12½ FL OZ/1½ CUPS)

SALSA di POMODORO e PISELLI

{ PEA AND TOMATO SALSA }

2 TEASPOONS OLIVE OIL

½ ONION, FINELY CHOPPED

1 CLOVE GARLIC, MINCED

PINCH OF CHILLI FLAKES

130 G (4½ OZ/1 CUP) FROZEN BABY PEAS

30 ML (1 FL OZ) DRY WHITE WINE

200 G (7 OZ) TINNED CHOPPED TOMATOES IN THEIR JUICE

1 TABLESPOON CHOPPED FLAT-LEAF PARSLEY LEAVES

This salsa uses ingredients that most people have in their pantries in all seasons. It is a good all-round vegetarian sauce for pasta, risotto or even on some soft creamy polenta.

Heat the oil in a saucepan over medium heat. Add the onion, then reduce the temperature to low and cook, stirring occasionally, for 12 minutes until soft and translucent. Add the garlic and chilli and cook until fragrant. Add the peas and cook for a few further minutes, then add the wine and increase the heat until the wine evaporates. Reduce the heat to low again, add the tomatoes, then stir and simmer, covered, for about 15 minutes. Add salt and pepper, to taste, remove from the heat and stir through the chopped parsley.

The salsa will keep in a ceramic or glass container, covered, in the fridge for 4–5 days.

MAKES ABOUT 375 ML (12½ FL OZ/1½ CUPS)

il SUGO di LIVIA

{ LIVIA'S MEAT SUGO }

60 ML (2 FL OZ/¼ CUP) OLIVE OIL

2 MEDIUM ONIONS, FINELY CHOPPED

1 SMALL—MEDIUM CARROT, FINELY DICED

1 CELERY STALK, FINELY DICED

1 GARLIC CLOVE, MINCED

500 G (1 LB 2 OZ) MINCED (GROUND) BEEF

250 ML (8½ FL OZ/1 CUP) RED WINE

600 G (1 LB 5 OZ) TINNED CHOPPED TOMATOES

1–2 TABLESPOONS GOOD-QUALITY TOMATO PURÉE (CONCENTRATED PURÉE)

¼ TEASPOON FRESHLY GRATED NUTMEG

1 FRESH BAY LEAF

2 TEASPOONS SALT

½ TEASPOON BLACK PEPPER

My mother Livia is nonna to four grandchildren. They all adore her meat sugo. She used to make it every week and whenever a family member came to visit, they would go home with some – even if they lived interstate and it had to go home on the plane. That's commitment to good food for you!

Heat the oil in a large heavy-based saucepan over low–medium heat. Add the onion and cook, stirring occasionally, for about 12 minutes until soft and translucent. Add the carrot, celery and garlic, and continue to cook for a further 12 minutes. Add the minced beef and cook, stirring occasionally to prevent it from sticking, until well browned. Add the wine and increase the heat to medium.

Cook for 10 minutes or until the liquid reduces by half. Reduce the heat to medium, then stir in the tomatoes and tomato purée. Add the nutmeg, bay leaf, salt and pepper. Cover, and simmer for about 1 hour, stirring occasionally. Adjust the salt and pepper, to taste.

The sugo will keep in a ceramic or glass container, covered, in the fridge for up to 1 week.

MAKES ABOUT 1 LITRE (34 FL OZ/4 CUPS)

INDEX

Affogato con cioccolata calda 250
almonds
    Neapolitan taralli 170
    Sweet Christmas taralli 188
anchovies
    Crostini with butter, anchovies
        and fresh mozzarella 52
    Crostini with egg and anchovy 41
    Crostini with whipped ricotta,
        anchovy and caperberries 45
    Fried mozzarella balls 93
    Spanish 41, 52
    Tomato and anchovy pizzette 33
    Truffled mushrooms, rocket and
        parmesan roll 104
    Zeppole with anchovies and
        olives 89
aniseed
    Potato fritters with aniseed 217
Apple fritters 201
Arancini con pomodoro e piselli 67
Arancini with tomatoes and peas 67
Arrosticini 151
artichokes, marinated
    Roman mortadella sandwich 111

Babà al rhum 191
baked goods 158–9
    Focaccia Bari-style 160
    Little taralli from Puglia 177
    Neapolitan taralli 170
    Onion and olive calzone 163
    Puffed cheese bites 169
    Rosemary buns 183
    Rustico pastry 174
    see also bread
bars and baristas 22–3
basil
    Peach and basil mascarpone ice
        cream 249
batter 75
Béchamel sauce 174
beef
    Beef stock 260
    Boiled meat picchiapò-style in a roll
        108, 260
    Fried meatballs 140
    Livia's meat sugo 265
    Nonna's little meatballs in a roll
        107

see also bresaola
Beef stock 260
Boiled meat picchiapò-style in a roll
    108, 260
Bombette Pugliesi 152
bread
    Fried bread balls 71
    Fried 'gnocchi' bread 147
    Fried mozzarella balls 93
    Pan-cooked flat bread 173
    Panzerotti 79
    Rosetta bread rolls 180
    see also panini
bresaola
    Crostini with pickled radicchio
        and bresaola 48
Brodo di carne 260
buns
    Rosemary buns 183
butter 52

Calzone con cipolla e olive 163
calzone
    Onion and olive calzone 163
cannoli
    Cocoa cannoli with ricotta 210
Cannoli al cacao con ricotta 210
caperberries
    Crostini with whipped ricotta,
        anchovy and caperberries 45
capers, rinsing 51
Cassatelle 195
Cassone verde 112
Castagnole con ricotta 224
cheese
    for cooking 18–19
    Crostini with Gorgonzola, pear and
        balsamic 42
    for eating 19
    Fried bread balls 71
    Gorgonzola and mushroom pizzette
        34
    Little meat bombs from Puglia 152
    Potato and cheese pancake 85
    Puffed cheese bites 169
    Truffled mushrooms, rocket and
        parmesan roll 104
    see also mozzarella; ricotta;
        scamorza
Chickpea fritters 90

Chickpea pancake with eggplant 98
Chicory polpette 80
chips
    Polenta chips 86
chocolate
    Hazelnut, chocolate and salted
        pistachio ice cream 244
    Hot chocolate with ice cream 250
Ciambelle 206
Cinque e cinque 98
Coccoli fritti 71
Cocoa cannoli with ricotta 210
Cozze fritte 129
Crema fritta 198
Crescentine 173
Crochette di patate 76
crostini 38
    Crostini with butter, anchovies and
        fresh mozzarella 52
    Crostini with egg and anchovy 41
    Crostini with Gorgonzola, pear and
        balsamic 42
    Crostini with mackerel pâté and
        capers 51
    Crostini with pickled radicchio and
        bresaola 48
    Crostini with whipped ricotta,
        anchovy and caperberries 45
    *Crostini con burro, acciughe
        e mozzarella* 52
    *Crostini con crema di sgombro
        e capperi* 51
    *Crostini con Gorgonzola, pera
        e balsamico* 42
    *Crostini con radicchio sottaceto
        e bresaola* 48
    *Crostini con ricotta mantecata,
        acciughe e frutti del cappero* 45
    Crostini con uova sode e acciughe 41
Crostoli 214
Crumbed mussels 129
Crumbed veal and lemon mayonnaise
    roll 101
custard
    Fried custard 198

dates
    Panettone ice cream 235
doughnuts
    Ring doughnuts 206

eggplant
  Chickpea pancake with eggplant 98
  Eggplant polpettine 58
eggs
  Crostini with egg and anchovy 41

fennel
  Porchetta roll 143
fennel seeds
  Little taralli from Puglia 177
Fiadoni Abruzzesi 169
Fiori di zucchini ripieni 75
fish and seafood 118
  Crostini with mackerel pâté and capers 51
  Crumbed mussels 129
  Grilled octopus 134
  Mixed fried fish in a cone 130
  Sardine polpette 120
  Stuffed sardines 119, 124
  Swordfish polpette 123
  unopened mussels 129
  Venetian-style sweet and sour sardines 133
flat bread
  Flat bread 'cassone' with greens 112
  Pan-cooked flat bread 173
flour (wheat) 17
Focaccia Barese 160
Focaccia Bari-style 160
Frico 85
Fried bread balls 71
Fried custard 198
Fried dough pockets 79
Fried 'gnocchi' bread 147
Fried meatballs 140
Fried mozzarella balls 93
Fried mozzarella sandwich 72
fried pasta 57
fried pizza 57
fried savoury snacks
  Arancini with tomatoes and peas 67
  Chicory polpette 80
  Eggplant polpettine 58
  Fried bread balls 71
  Fried dough pockets 79
  Fried mozzarella balls 93
  Fried mozzarella sandwich 72
  fried pasta 57
  fried pizza 57
  Polenta chips 86
  Potato croquettes 57, 76

Stuffed zucchini flowers in batter 75
Supplì with meat ragù 63
Zeppole with anchovies and olives 89
see also fritters
Fritole Triestine 201
fritters
  Apple fritters 201
  Chickpea fritters 90
  Potato and cheese pancake 85
  Potato fritters with aniseed 217
Fritto misto di pesce in cono 130
frying, open-air 56-7

Garlic mayonnaise 257
Gelato al panettone 235
Gelato alla nocciola, e cioccolato con pistacchi salati 244
Gelato alla pesca e basilico 249
Gelato di crema ai sette sapori 230
Gelato di pere e acqua di rose 243
Gelato di ricotta e limone 236
Gnocchi fritti 147
Gorgonzola and mushroom pizzette 34
grapefruit
  Orange, pink grapefruit and Aperol sorbet 240
Grilled lamb bites 151
Grilled octopus 134

Hazelnut, chocolate and salted pistachio ice cream 244
honey
  Sardinian ricotta cakes 223
  Hot chocolate with ice cream 250

ice creams and sorbets 228-9
  Hazelnut, chocolate and salted pistachio ice cream 244
  Hot chocolate with ice cream 250
  Orange, pink grapefruit sorbet with Aperol 240
  Panettone ice cream 235
  Peach and basil mascarpone ice cream 249
  Pear and rosewater ice cream 243
  Plum and amaretto sorbet 239
  Ricotta and lemon ice cream 236
  serving 230
  Spiced crema ice cream 230
Il sugo di Livia 265

lamb
  Grilled lamb bites 151
leeks
  Onion and olive calzone 163
lemon
  Cassatelle 195
  Lemon mayonnaise 256
  Lemon taralli 218
  Ricotta and lemon ice cream 236
  Sardinian ricotta cakes 223
Little meat bombs from Puglia 152
Little taralli from Puglia 177
Livia's meat sugo 265
Luganega con aceto 154

Mackerel crema 51
mackerel mayonnaise 51
mackerel pâté 51
  Crostini with mackerel pâté and capers 51
mackerel, tinned 51
Maionnese al limone 256
Maionnese all'aglio 257
mascarpone
  Peach and basil mascarpone ice cream 249
mayonnaise
  Garlic mayonnaise 257
  Lemon mayonnaise 256
  Mackerel 'crema' 51
meat
  Boiled meat picchiapò-style in a roll 108, 260
  Grilled lamb bites 151
  Little meat bombs from Puglia 152
  Porchetta roll 143
  Pork sausage bites 154
  Stuffed fried olives 144
  see also beef
meatballs
  Fried meatballs 140
  Nonna's little meatballs in a roll 107
Mixed fried fish in a cone 130
mortadella
  Roman mortadella sandwich 111
mozzarella 18-19, 79
  Crostini with butter, anchovies and fresh mozzarella 52
  Fried mozzarella balls 93
  Fried mozzarella sandwich 72
  Potato croquettes 57, 76
  Sausage, zucchini and mozzarella pizzette 37

Supplì with meat ragù 63
Tomato and mozzarella
    pizzette 27
Mozzarella fritta 93
mushrooms
    Gorgonzola and mushroom
        pizzette 34
    Truffled mushrooms, rocket and
        parmesan roll 104
mussels
    Crumbed mussels 129
    unopened 129

Neapolitan taralli 170
Nonna's little meatballs in a
    roll 107
nuts
    Hazelnut, chocolate and salted
        pistachio ice cream 244
    Sweet Christmas taralli 188
    see also almonds

octopus
    boiled 119
    Grilled octopus 134
    preparing 134
oil
    rosemary 183
    testing temperature 224
Olive all'ascolane 144
olives
    Focaccia Bari-style 160
    Onion and olive calzone 163
    Stuffed fried olives 144
    Zeppole with anchovies and
        olives 89
onions
    Onion and olive calzone 163
    Potato and onion pizzette 28
    Venetian-style sweet and sour
        sardines 133
orange
    Orange, pink grapefruit and Aperol
        sorbet 240
    Panettone ice cream 235
    Ring doughnuts 206
    Rum baba 191
    Sardinian ricotta cakes 223
    Stuffed sardines 119, 124

Pan di ramerino 183
pancakes, savoury
    Chickpea pancake with eggplant
        98

Potato and cheese pancake
    85
Pan-cooked flat bread 173
Panelle 90
Panettone ice cream 235
panini 96–7
    Boiled meat picchiapò-style in a roll
        108, 260
    Chickpea pancake with eggplant
        98
    Crumbed veal and lemon
        mayonnaise roll 101
    Flat bread 'cassone' with greens
        112
    Nonna's little meatballs in a roll
        107
    Porchetta roll 143
    Roman mortadella sandwich 111
    Truffled mushrooms, rocket and
        parmesan roll 104
Panino con fettine impanate e
    maionnese al limone 101
Panino con lesso alla picchiapò 108,
    260
Panino con polpettine della nonna 107
Panino con porchetta 143
*Panino con tartufata, rucola e
    parmigiano* 104
Panzerotti 79
Pardule 223
pasta, fried 57
pastry
    Rustico pastry 174
    Shortcrust pastry sfogliatelle 202,
        205
Peach and basil mascarpone ice
    cream 249
pears
    Crostini with Gorgonzola, pear and
        balsamic 42
    Pear and rosewater ice cream 243
peas
    Arancini with tomatoes and peas
        67
    Pea and tomato salsa 262
Pisto 188
pizza
    fried pizza 57
    Roman mortadella sandwich 111
pizzette
    dough 24
    Gorgonzola and mushroom pizzette
        34
    Potato and onion pizzette 28

Sausage, zucchini and mozzarella
    pizzette 37
Tomato and anchovy pizzette 33
Tomato and mozzarella pizzette 27
Pizzette con Gorgonzola e funghi 34
Pizzette con patate e cipolle 28
Pizzette con pomodoro e acciughe 33
Pizzette con pomodoro e mozzarella 27
*Pizzette con salsicce, zucchine e
    mozzarella* 37
Plum and amaretto sorbet 239
Polpetta di cicoria 80
Polpette di pesce spada 123
Polpette di sarde 120
Polpettine di bar 140
Polpettine di melanzane 58
Polpo alla griglia 134
porchetta 138–9
    Porchetta roll 143
pork
    crackling 143
    Little meat bombs from Puglia 152
    Pork sausage bites 154
potatoes
    Focaccia Bari-style 160
    Potato and cheese pancake 85
    Potato croquettes 57, 76
    Potato fritters with aniseed 217
    Potato and onion pizzette 28
    Zeppole with anchovies and olives
        89
prosciutto
    Fried bread balls 71
    Puffed cheese bites 169

radicchio
    Crostini with pickled radicchio and
        bresaola 48
    pickling 48
Raviole Bolognesi 209
rice
    Arancini with tomatoes and peas
        67
    Supplì with meat ragù 63
ricotta 18
    Cocoa cannoli with ricotta 210
    Crostini with whipped ricotta,
        anchovy and caperberries 45
    Potato fritters with aniseed 217
    Ricotta and lemon ice cream 236
    Sardinian ricotta cakes 223
    Shortcrust pastry sfogliatelle 202,
        205

Stuffed zucchini flowers in batter 75
Sweet ricotta balls 224
Ring doughnuts 206
Risotto 63
    Arancini with tomatoes and peas 67
    Supplì with meat ragù 63
rocket
    Truffled mushrooms, rocket and parmesan roll 104
Rococò 188
Roman mortadella sandwich 111
rosemary
    Porchetta roll 143
    Rosemary buns 183
    Rosemary oil 183
Rosetta bread rolls 180
Rosette di pane 180
rosewater
    Pear and rosewater ice cream 243
Rum baba 191
Rustico Leccese 174
Rustico pastry 174

Salsa di pomodoro 261
Salsa di pomodoro e piselli 262
salsa
    Pea and tomato salsa 262
    Simple tomato salsa 261
sandwich
    Fried mozzarella sandwich 72
    Roman mortadella sandwich 111
Sarde a beccafico 119, 124
Sarde in sa'or 119, 133
sardines
    Sardine polpette 120
    Stuffed sardines 119, 124
    Venetian-style sweet and sour sardines 119, 133
Sardinian ricotta cakes 223
sauces and basics
    Béchamel sauce 174
    Beef stock 260
    Garlic mayonnaise 257
    Lemon mayonnaise 256
    Livia's meat sugo 265
    Pea and tomato salsa 262
    Simple tomato salsa 261
sausage
    Pork sausage bites 154
    Roman mortadella sandwich 111
    Sausage, zucchini and mozzarella pizzette 37
Scagliozzi 86

scamorza 19
seafood
    see fish and seafood
semolina 17
Sfogliatelle con pasta frolla 202, 205
Shortcrust pastry sfogliatelle 202, 205
Simple tomato salsa 261
skewers
    Little meat bombs from Puglia 152
    Stuffed sardines 119, 124
sorbets
    see ice creams and sorbets
Sorbetto all'arancia, pompelmo rosa e Aperol 240
Sorbetto alle susine di amaretto 239
Spanish anchovies 41, 52
spices
    Pisto 188
    Spiced crema ice cream 230
spinach
    Flat bread 'cassone' with greens 112
stock
    , Beef stock 260
street food 10–15
strutto (pork fat) 210
Stuffed fried olives 144
Stuffed sardines 119, 124
Stuffed zucchini flowers in batter 75
Sugar syrup 183
sugo
    Livia's meat sugo 265
    Supplì al telefono con ragù 63
    Supplì with meat ragù 63
Sweet Christmas taralli 188
Sweet fried pastries with lemon ricotta 195
Sweet fried pastry wings 214
Sweet pastry raviole 209
Sweet ricotta balls 224
sweet treats
    Apple fritters 201
    Cocoa cannoli with ricotta 210
    Fried custard 198
    Lemon taralli 218
    Potato fritters with aniseed 217
    Ring doughnuts 206
    Rum baba 191
    Sardinian ricotta cakes 223
    Shortcrust pastry sfogliatelle 202, 203
    Sweet Christmas taralli 188
    Sweet fried pastries with lemon ricotta 195

Sweet fried pastry wings 214
Sweet pastry raviole 209
Sweet ricotta balls 224
Swordfish polpette 123

Taralli al limone 218
Taralli Napoletani 170
taralli
    Lemon taralli 218
    Little taralli from Puglia 177
    Neapolitan taralli 170
    Sweet Christmas taralli 188
Tarallini Pugliesi 177
tomato
    Arancini with tomatoes and peas 67
    Boiled meat picchiapò-style in a roll 108, 260
    Focaccia Bari-style 160
    Livia's meat sugo 265
    Panzerotti 79
    Pea and tomato salsa 262
    Rustico pastry 174
    Simple tomato salsa 261
    Tomato and mozzarella pizzette 27
Torcinelli 217
Truffled mushrooms, rocket and parmesan roll 104

veal
    Crumbed veal and lemon mayonnaise roll 101
Venetian-style sweet and sour sardines 133

yeast 17–18

Zeppole con acciughe e olive 89
Zeppole with anchovies and olives 89
zucchini
    Sausage, zucchini and mozzarella pizzette 37
zucchini flowers
    Stuffed zucchini flowers in batter 75

ACKNOWLEDGEMENTS

THIS BOOK IS DEDICATED TO MY MOTHER LIVIA, MY CONSTANT SOURCE OF INSPIRATION AND THE PERSON WHO TAUGHT ME ABOUT THE IMPORTANCE OF TRADITIONAL RECIPES, COOKING FROM SCRATCH AND THE FAMILY TABLE.

THANK YOU

Thank you to Mark for his patience, love, support and for happily eating street food daily for several months while I tested recipes; Tamara for being a wonderful and encouraging daughter; my family – Barbara, Claire and my aunts and uncles in Italy for being there, feeding me at various times and believing that I could do this; Ben, for cooking beside me over the years and encouraging me in my food journey; friends in Italy – Alice, Giulia, Maria, Rachel, Toni and especially to Emiko for generously sharing her knowledge; Paolo and Verdiana for tasting the food and giving feedback over a game (or five) of Briscola; friends Lisa, Ian, Jo, Nicole and Matt for your encouragement and support; work colleagues Deb, Sue, Andrea, Pam and Louise who shared my excitement for the project; staff at Smith Street Books who believed I could do this and helped me finish the project on time – Paul McNally, Lucy Heaver, Murray Batten; Sarah Schembri, Trish Gallagher and Anthony Julius for the wonderful plates and food styling backgrounds; Ian Summers for the additional photos; all my blog readers and social media followers on *Italy on my mind* for encouraging comments and for following my journey; my wonderful recipe testers without whom I could not have done this – Christine Menegazzo, Bronie Duncan, Suzana Borovan, Gabrielle Schaffner, Cori Williams, Jessica Fransson, Sharon O'Donnell, Carmen Pricone, Cristina Pepe, Nell Hunderford, Eleanor Dempster, Paula Barbarito-Levitt, Liliana Pellizzon, Ronnie Pellizzon, Katie Pepper, David Scott Allen, Mariko Chan, Emma Verri, Annette Guyatt, Merry Canavan, Vanessa Miles, Roshena Campbell, Loretta Swayn, Pia Beltrame, Claire Peck, Laura Ivy, Carolina D'Angelo, Emma Gallagher, Phyllis de Jong-White, Dolores Leropoulos, Janie Treyer, Amanda Alacqua and Karen Williams.

Published in 2016 by Smith Street Books
Melbourne | Australia
smithstreetbooks.com

ISBN: 978-1-9254-1818-7

CIP data is available from the National Library of Australia

Publisher: Paul McNally
Senior editor: Lucy Heaver, Tusk studio
Designer: Murray Batten
Typesetter: Kate Barraclough

Printed & bound in China by C&C Offset Printing Co., Ltd.

Book 18
10 9 8 7 6 5 4 3 2 1